Contents

Encouraging Topic Interest

Help students to develop an understanding and appreciation of different media concepts by encouraging them to bring in examples of media to create a class display. You may also wish to conduct and display class surveys on media topics, or to compare students' media preferences.

Vocabulary List

Students can use the **Media Literacy Vocabulary** blackline master to record new vocabulary or theme-related words. In addition, new and theme-related vocabulary can be listed on chart paper for students to refer to during writing activities. During each new activity, encourage students to suggest words to add to the list. Classify the word list into the categories of nouns, verbs, and adjectives.

Blackline Masters and Graphic Organizers

Use the blackline masters and graphic organizers in this book as appropriate for the level of your students. These reproducibles can be used to present information, reinforce important media concepts, and to extend opportunities for learning. The graphic organizers will also help students focus on important ideas, and make direct comparisons.

Learning Logs

Keeping a learning log is an effective way for students to organize their thoughts and ideas about the social studies concepts presented. Students' learning logs also provide insight on what follow-up activities are needed to review and clarify concepts learned.

Learning logs can include the following types of entries:

• Teacher prompts
• Students' personal reflections
• Questions that arise
• Connections discovered
• Labeled diagrams and pictures

Rubrics and Checklists

Use the rubrics and checklists in this book to assess students' learning.

Introduction to Media

From an early age, children are exposed to all types of media including billboards, logos, brand names, Internet ads, and television- and movie-character merchandise. These images and the messages they carry can influence, and have an impact on, the minds of young children.

Understanding how to read and write media is a critical asset for children of this generation to learn. Young children need to build skills that will help them identify, assess, and critique information presented to them in various forms of media. In the early years, learning how to create media is a fun and engaging way to talk about the characteristics of media and its various forms.

Investigating big ideas through the use of media is a great way for students to get excited about learning and to stay engaged. In any subject area, aspects of media can be incorporated into classroom topics and discussions in interesting and engaging ways.

Making Sense of the World

As students learn to make sense of the world around them, they also learn to make meaningful connections to the media to which they are exposed. By using examples from their world—what is viewed, read, and listened to—students can learn to make sense of media in a way that is meaningful to them.

Parents can help their children learn about media. Talking about media at home helps children recognize various media forms, such as an advertisement, a cartoon, or a website. This is a first step toward making children aware of the types of media around them and the many ways that media is presented. Parents and teachers need to work together to help children become aware of, and critical of, the things they learn, read, and play with.

This resource explores how to teach media in the classroom, and how to recognize it in the real world. Through activities such as creating media, deconstructing media, and reading and writing media texts, *Media Literacy Activities K–3* helps students build essential skills and knowledge to succeed in the 21st century.

What Is Media Literacy?

Background Information

Definitions of *media literacy* vary widely and often include the following abilities:

- To understand and interpret media texts
- To identify a variety of media forms
- To recognize techniques used in media texts and understand the impacts of these techniques
- To communicate effectively using a variety of media forms

Critical thinking skills are a key part of media literacy. Students learn to become critical media "consumers" and effective media creators by actively questioning media texts. Students will also understand the influence media texts have on various individuals and groups, as well as society.

Media literacy is a learned skill that requires consistent opportunities to practice. The questions below can be used for any type of media text examined.

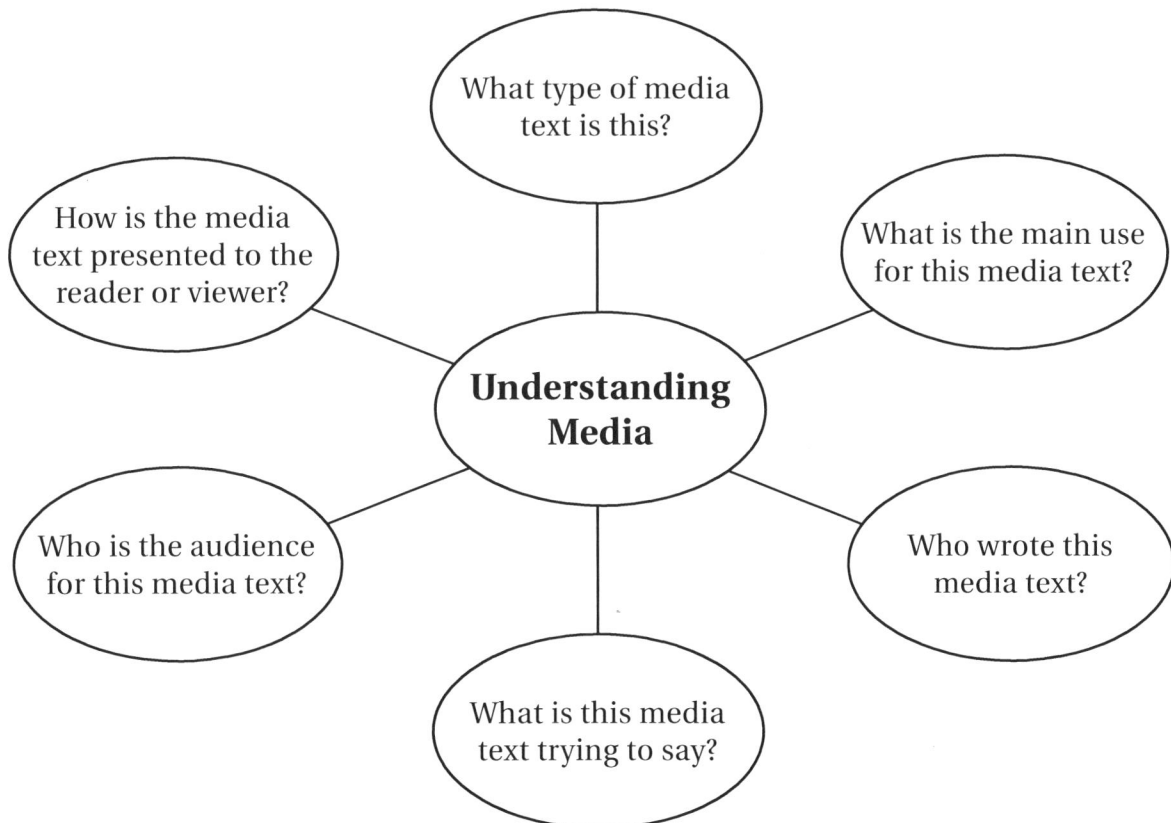

What type of media text is this?

How is the media text presented to the reader or viewer?

What is the main use for this media text?

Understanding Media

Who is the audience for this media text?

Who wrote this media text?

What is this media text trying to say?

Introducing Media

Background Information

Media: Usually used to collectively refer to the most common forms of mass communication, including television, radio, newspapers, and the Internet.

Media form: The form used to communicate a message. Media forms include print forms such as a novel or brochure, and a wide variety of non-print forms as a blog, movie, podcast, television news broadcast, and product packaging.

Print media: This term is sometimes defined as any media text that is produced on paper, often through the use of a printing press. However, there are many other examples of print media, including a transparency, a blimp with a company logo, and texts that are handwritten or printed from a computer. A print media text does not always contain words. For example, a photograph printed on paper is a print media text.

Digital media: Electronic devices and media platforms on which people can create and store media texts, and interact with other people, the device, or the actual application. Digital media includes computers, cell phones, digital cameras, the Internet, social networking websites, and video games. Digital media texts may include sound, still images, animations, photographs, and video.

Media text: Any text, image, sound, or visual representation (or any combination of two or more of these) used to communicate a message. Note that while many media texts do contain spoken or written words, some do not; for example, a photograph and a painting are each considered to be a media text.

Media text features: Characteristics of a text that clarify the text, including fonts, headings, and illustrations.

Media conventions and techniques: Creating specific effects using images and sounds to convey the message in a text. Examples of effects include using animation, color, logos, special effects, and more.

Introducing Media—Activity Ideas

I Read, Look At, Watch, and Listen To...

1. Ask students to look around the room and identify anything in the room that they read, look at, watch, or listen to. They might identify such things as books, charts, photographs, drawings, magazine pictures, computer games, television, or CD player. For devices such as a television, ask students to identify how they use the device. For example, students might say they use the television to watch movies and children's shows. Keep track of responses on the board. Expand the list to include anything that they read, looked at, watched, or listened to since they got up in the morning. For example, students might mention cereal boxes, street signs, or comic books. Record all examples.

2. On the board, print the headings "Words," "Pictures," and "Sounds." Ask students to categorize under these headings the items from their list in the activity above. They will soon realize that many are a combination of two or more. Add headings as needed. For example, you might add the headings "Words and pictures," or "Pictures and sounds." Explain that media is anything we read, look at, watch, or listen to. Encourage students to give examples of other types of media they know. Add their examples as students discover more.

Identifying Media Forms

1. In a whole-group setting, display examples of media such as a newspaper, magazine, DVD, brochure, menu, print advertisement, sign, and an open Internet site for students to view.

2. Display items one at a time to students and ask, "What is this?" When necessary, rephrase students' responses to focus on the fact that it is an example of media. For example, if a student says, "That is an ad for cereal," respond with, "Yes, this is an example of media." After students have responded to all the items, confirm with them that they have been identifying examples of media.

3. Reinforce that media is all things they read, look at, watch, and listen to. Also reinforce that all media give some type of message with a purpose. Revisit each item and record students' responses on chart paper as the following questions are asked:

   • What is this called?
   • How do we know this is media? Is it something we read, look at, watch, or listen to?
   • What is the message?

My Media Book

For younger students, use **BLM 12: My Media Book**. Have students cut out the pages and put them in numerical order. Check the order before stapling the books for students. Read each page of the book with students, or invite individual students to read a page each. After you read the related media page, you might wish to ask students to share with the class the name of their favorite book, song, etc. Students may also use the back of each page of the booklet to list their favorite examples.

Media Walk

1. As a class, walk around your school and neighborhood. Make a list of all the media forms spotted. These might include community signs, billboards, displays, posters, books, etc. Talk about how each of these media examples gives a message.

2. Next, provide students with magazines, sale ads, and advertisements. Have students cut out pictures to create a media forms collage using **BLM 13: Media Collage**.

Messages Without Words

Help students recognize that messages can be communicated without using words, such as through symbols and photographs. Give opportunities for students to look at a variety of symbols and associate a message. In addition, show students several photographs and ask them to explain what they perceive the message to be. Brainstorm a list of reasons of why people take photographs and why we have symbols around the community.

What Is Digital Media?

1. As a class, brainstorm a list of commonly used digital media devices, such as laptops, mobile phones, tablets, touchscreen music players, etc. You may also wish to include digital media storage devices, such as external hard drives, flash drives, portable music players, CDs, and DVDs.

2. Review with students the list of digital devices created in the last step. If students have created an extensive list, choose a few items to focus on. For each item, ask the following questions:

    • In what way can you share your ideas with other people using this device?
    • Do you have any experience using this device?
    • What do you think would happen if a person did not have this device?
    • How often do you read a story on the computer? What is an ebook?
    • Do you prefer reading a story as an ebook or a regular book? Why?

Exploring Online Media

In this ever-changing world, it essential for children to become media savvy and familiar with online media. As children are introduced to the Internet, usually by a family member or caregiver, they begin to master navigating skills and become more independent. Children can visit websites related to their favorite toys, television shows, books, music, and movies. They can play games online that may include a virtual world where they can communicate with other children. The Internet allows access to great child-friendly learning games and educational websites. However, students must learn the basics of Internet safety and how to protect themselves.

As an introduction, ask students if the Internet is a real place. Explore students' reasoning for their answers. Then make sure students understand that the Internet is not a real place—not like a farm or a library that people can visit. Yet, the Internet is made up of billions of people who can connect with each other through computers even though they are not in the same place.

As a whole group, further explore the Internet with students. Ask students to suggest ways other people or they at home use the Internet. Students may suggest downloading and listening to music, watching videos, visiting favorite sites, or emailing people. Review how to navigate the computer and reinforce proper vocabulary such as *search engine*. You may also wish to ask students the following questions:

- Who do you go online with? Are you allowed to go online by yourself?
- What types of things do you like to do online?
- Can you go online whenever you want to, or are there rules?
- What video games do you like to play? Why?
- Would you rather play with toys, or would you rather play a video game online? Why?

Staying Safe Online

It is essential for students to learn how to go online safely. As a class, brainstorm a list of rules that students follow when they go somewhere. Start with examples such as a school field trip or going to the store with their family. Emphasize that these rules help to keep students safe. Then talk about how they are also visiting places when they go on the Internet, so they need to follow rules to stay safe. Stress the following rules:

1. Only visit websites that an adult says are safe.
2. Only visit a website with permission from an adult.
3. Do not talk to strangers online!

Sending Messages

1. Brainstorm with students the different ways people send and receive messages. Students may suggest writing notes and sticky notes, mailing letters and cards, making phone calls, creating and posting signs, instant messaging, and sending emails and text messages.

2. Inform students that email is a way for people to send each other messages through the Internet. Email travels from the computer of the person who sent it, through the Internet, to the computer of the person who they sent it to. Email and text messages are similar, but text messages are always very short whereas emails can be a lot longer. Text messaging generally consists of short messages with abbreviated words such as "LOL" for "Laughing Out Loud," "u" for "you," and "G2G" for "Got to Go." Because text messages must be short, the language is abbreviated to save space.

3. Ask students the following questions to find out what they know about email:

   • Have you ever sent anyone an email? What did you like or not like about sending an email?
   • Have you ever received an email? What did you like or not like about receiving and reading an email?
   • What are some of the reasons people might want to send emails?
   • Do you think email is faster or slower than mailing a letter through the post office? Why?
   • Have you ever seen anyone send a text message?
   • Are the same devices used to send text messages and emails? What devices are used for each?

Media Form Riddle Cards

1. Have students work with a partner to play a game that tests their knowledge of media forms. Have students cut out the cards on **BLM 14: Media Form Riddle Cards.**

2. Partner A chooses one card and reads the clues aloud to Partner B. Partner B then tries to guess the media form from the clues provided. Partner A checks the answer at the bottom of the card, and says whether the guess is correct or incorrect. If Partner B guessed incorrectly, they are allowed one more guess. If their second guess is incorrect, students then switch roles and Partner B chooses the next clue card to read to Partner A.

3. Students keep choosing new cards and guessing until all the cards are finished.

Media Forms Word Search

T	P	O	S	T	E	R	W	E	C
B	I	L	L	B	O	A	R	D	O
E	A	S	T	B	O	O	K	W	M
M	D	O	S	I	G	N	A	E	M
A	W	N	S	M	E	N	U	B	E
P	S	G	C	O	M	I	C	S	R
P	I	C	T	U	R	E	T	I	C
M	A	G	A	Z	I	N	E	T	I
E	C	A	R	D	A	S	T	E	A
N	E	W	S	P	A	P	E	R	L

sign   book   ad   magazine
comic   map   song   commercial
poster   website   card   billboard
menu   picture   newspaper

BLM 1

Media Every Day

We see and hear media every day. Media gives us messages. Some media messages we see. Some media messages we hear. Some media messages we read. The pictures show some types of media.

books	cartoons	songs	commercials
newspapers	websites	ads	street signs

Think About It!

Media Every Day

1. List more examples of media.

_____

_____

2. Describe the ways you see and hear media every day.

_____

_____

_____

BLM 2

Television Is Media

There are different types of shows on television. There are cartoons, news shows, stories, game shows, and much more! Many shows have commercials. A television show and a commercial are different.

Commercial	**Television Show**
• It is very short.	• It is long.
• It sells a product.	• It gives information or entertains.

Television Is Media

Think About It!

1. What are the clues that tell you what you are watching?

a) Clues that tell me I am watching a cartoon:

_____

_____

b) Clues that tell me I am watching a news show:

_____

_____

c) Clues that tell me I am watching a commercial:

_____

_____

All About Media Forms

Media All Around Us

We see and hear media every day. The things we see on television are media. Books are media. Signs we see in the community are media. Songs we hear on the radio are media. There are many different types of media. We can put media into groups called **media forms**.

Media Forms on Television

There are many different types of shows on television. Here are some of the different types:

• Cartoons • News shows • Game shows

Cartoons, news shows, and game shows are all different media forms. Most television shows have commercials. Commercials are another media form we see on television. Commercials are very short.

Media Forms in Books

There are many different types of books. Here are some of the different types:

• Picture books • Coloring books • Dictionaries

These different types of books are all different media forms.

continued next page ☞

BLM 4

Other Media Forms

Around the community we see signs. Signs are one type of media form. Some signs, such as stop signs, do not have words but give us information about what to do. Other signs, such as traffic signs and billboards, have words. Maps are a type of media form that tells us where places are located.

Fastest car this year!

Think About It!

All About Media Forms

1. What is media? Use information from the reading and your own ideas to write your answer.

_____

_____

_____

_____

2. Coloring books and picture books both contain pictures. What are two ways that coloring books and picture books are different?

_____

_____

_____

Signs and Symbols

1. Look at the examples below. Explain what message each of these signs or symbols send us.

a) _____ _____ _____

b) _____ _____ _____

c) _____ _____ _____

d) _____ _____ _____

e) _____ _____ _____

f) _____ _____ _____

g) _____ _____ _____

h) _____ _____ _____

2. Draw a sign or symbol and explain its message.

_____

_____

BLM 5

A Picture Gives a Message

Cut and a paste a photograph or a picture from a magazine into the space below.

What message does the photograph or picture give us?

_____

What are the clues?

_____

_____

What Is the Internet?

The Internet is made up of computers all around the world. These computers are connected by telephone lines or cables. The Internet lets computers communicate with one another. A computer that has an Internet connection can do two things:

• Send information to other computers that are part of the Internet

• Receive information sent by other computers on the Internet

Not every computer is connected to the Internet. People have to pay money each month to have their computer connected to the Internet.

How Do People Use the Internet?

When people go online, they are connected to the Internet. Here are some different ways people use the Internet:

• To learn information from websites

• To play computer games

• To share information and photographs with others

• To send and receive messages such as emails and text messages

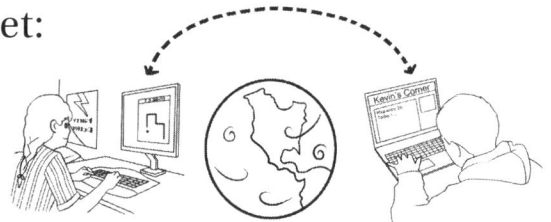

• To shop for things

Cell Phones and the Internet

Some cell phones can connect to the Internet. That means people can receive and send information over the Internet by using a cell phone instead of a computer.

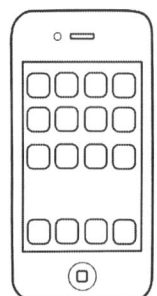

BLM 7

What Is the Internet?

1. You have probably used a computer at home or at school to look at websites on the Internet. Name two topics that you have learned about by looking at Internet websites.

Topic 1: _____

Topic 2: _____

2. If you have a computer with Internet at home, tell two things you use the Internet to do. If you are not connected to the Internet at home, tell two ways that you would like to use the Internet.

_____

_____

_____

_____

3. People can send an email or a text message to just about any place in the world. There are two other ways people can communicate with someone who is far away. What are these two ways, and which way is faster?

_____

_____

_____

_____

Websites I Recommend

Website	Purpose of Website	Why I Like the Website

Websites I Recommend

1. Go online with an adult. Find a website you like. Draw a picture of what you see on the website. Complete the sentence.

The website tells about _____

2. Put a check mark for each safety rule you follow online.

☐ I go only to websites that an adult says are safe.

☐ I talk only with people I know.

We Send and Receive Messages

An *email* is a message we write and send on the computer. The message is something we want to ask or tell someone. We write messages for many reasons. We wish someone a happy day. We share news. Sometimes we make plans.

Do you want to go to the park?

The email travels through the Internet. It goes from your computer to the computer of your friend. She *receives* the message.

Yes, I can go today!

BLM 9

Think About It!

Jane and Tom are using email.

Message 1
From: Jane
To: Tom
Subject: Movie
I want to see a movie. Which movie is your favorite?
Jane

Message 2
From: Tom
To: Jane
Subject: Movie
I like Animals Gone Wild. It is very funny.
Tom

Message 3
From: Jane
To: Tom
Subject: Movie
Thank you Tom. I will try to go.
Jane

1. Circle the answer.

   a) Who sent Message 1?   Jane   Tom

   b) Who received Message 2?   Jane   Tom

   c) Who received Message 3?   Jane   Tom

Activity: Sending Email

Write an email message to a friend or someone in your family. Draw a picture of you sending the message and of the person who will receive the message. Label the drawing. Use the words below.

email   **Internet**   **receive**   **send**

Media in-a-Day Tally

1. Carefully record the examples of media you see, watch, or listen to in one day. Share your results with the class and compare.

Media	Tally
Television	
Radio	
Internet	
Book	
Newspaper	
Ad	
Brochure	
Comic	
Blog	
Movie	
Music	
Poster	
Billboard	
Logo	
Menu	
Other	

2. Look at the results. What do you think of your results?

_____

_____

My Media Book

_____'s Book

1

I read books.

We see and hear media every day.

2

BLM 12

I watch television.

Eat your vegetables!

We see and hear media every day.

3

I look at signs.

RESTROOM

We see and hear media every day.

4

BLM 12

I read and look at comics.

We see and hear media every day.

5

I listen to songs.

We see and hear media every day.

6

I look at pictures.

We see and hear media every day.

7

I go on the Internet.

Kevin's Corner

Blog entry 24:
Today I....

We hear and see media every day.

8

I draw pictures.

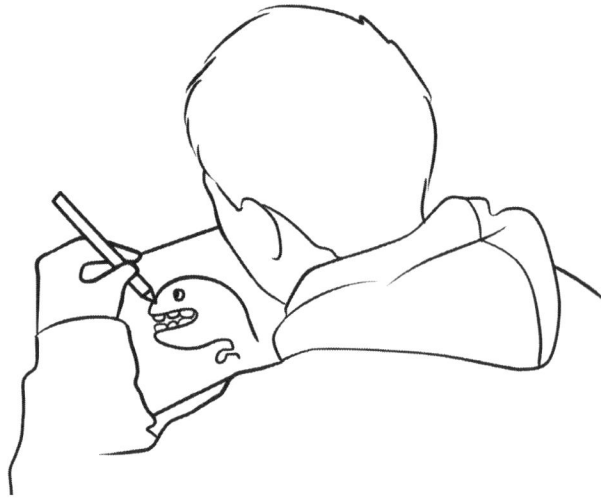

We see and hear media every day.

9

Media is all around us.

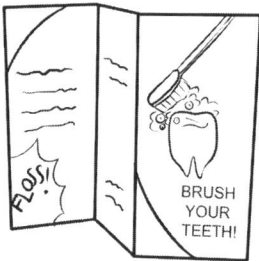

FLOSS!

BRUSH YOUR TEETH!

We hear and see media every day.

10

BLM 12

Media Collage

1. Look through magazines to find examples of media. Cut out the
pictures and paste them in the space below to make a collage.

2. Write about your collage:

_____

_____

Media Form Riddle Cards

1

Media form clues:

I am made of large sheets of paper.

I have photographs and lots of words.

I tell people the news.

What am I?

Answer: A newspaper

2

Media form clues:

I am a book that does not tell a story.

You use me to find out what different words mean.

What am I?

Answer: A dictionary

3

Media form clues:

I am a special type of television show.

I tell you about what is happening in the world.

I also tell you what the weather is going to be like.

What am I?

Answer: A television news show

4

Media form clues:

I am a book that has recipes for making different foods.

I tell you what ingredients you need, and what you have to do.

What am I?

Answer: A cookbook

continued next page ☞

BLM 14

Media form clues: 5

I am a folded piece of thick paper.

You put me in an envelope.

You give me to someone on special occasions such as a birthday.

What am I?

Answer: A greeting card

Media form clues: 6

To find me, people use a computer and go on the Internet.

I can give information about many different topics.

I can have words, pictures, and sometimes videos.

What am I?

Answer: A website

Media form clues: 7

You see lots of me on television.

I am shorter than a television show, and I tell you about different things you can buy.

What am I?

Answer: A television commercial

Media form clues: 8

I am a big picture on a piece of paper.

Sometimes I show different countries and sometimes I show the streets in a city.

I can help you find your way if you are lost.

What am I?

Answer: A map

continued next page ☞

BLM 14

Media form clues:

9

I have lots of pages with words and pictures, but I am not a book or a newspaper.

You can buy me at a store, but some people get me in the mail.

What am I?

Answer: A magazine

Media form clues:

10

I am a huge poster that is much taller than you.

You see me on the sides of buildings and along roads.

I am like a commercial on paper.

What am I?

Answer: A billboard

Media form clues:

11

I am a special type of book that children like.

I tell a story. I also have pictures that show what is happening in the story.

What am I?

Answer: A picture book

Media form clues:

12

I have words and music.

Sometimes you hear me on the radio. "The Star-Spangled Banner" is one example of me.

What am I?

Answer: A song

BLM 14

Examining Print Text Features

As a class, examine print texts such as a textbook, dictionary, picture book, comic book, newspaper, magazine, poster, non-fiction book, fiction book, and brochure. For example,

Non-fiction book: Explain that these books are designed so that it is easy to find information. Some text features may include a contents page, glossary, captions, diagrams, subheadings, chapter titles, and pictures with labels. For younger students, you may refer to a text feature as a "reader's tool." Use the following questions as discussion starters:

• How does an illustration or a photograph help you understand what you are reading?
• How does a labelled diagram help you understand the explanation?
• What is the purpose of a glossary in a non-fiction book? How does it help the reader?
• How do you use the table of contents?

Newspaper: Encourage students to explore the parts of the newspaper, then have a general discussion. Introduce vocabulary such as *headline*, *section*, *byline*, etc. For example,

• How do you find out what information is inside the newspaper?
• Why do you think people read newspapers?
• Which headline on the front page is the largest?
• Why do you think some stories are longer than others?

Conduct a class scavenger hunt for print text features in the newspaper. For example,

• Name a section of the newspaper. • Find the comics section.
• Find the weather forecast. • Find an advertisement.

Picture book: Discuss with students how pictures and fonts help tell the story and establish the mood of a picture book. Explain that these choices were made by the author and illustrator. Here are some discussion starters:

• How do you feel when you look at this picture? Explain why.
• What has the illustrator done to make you feel this way?
• What colors seem important in this picture? Why do they seem important?
• How do the colors in this picture make you feel? Explain why.

Poster: Ask students what posters they are familiar with. Students may suggest movie posters, wanted posters from books and television shows, posters about community events. Review with students the parts of a typical poster: has a title, or heading; usually has one message; pictures are a large part of the poster; and it can be read quickly.

Features in a Print Text

Use this page to identify the features you find in a print text, and explain how each feature helps readers.

Print text: _____

Feature	How the Feature Helps Readers

BLM 15

Examining Media Texts

Background Information

Purpose

There are three main purposes of media texts: to *inform*, to *entertain*, and to *persuade*.

Many media texts are created to inform people—to provide them with information. A television news broadcast and a newspaper both inform people about what is happening in their local community, their country, and the world.

Many media texts have the purpose of persuading people to do something, such as buy a particular product or give money to a certain charity.

Many media texts are created to entertain people. Movie trailers, music videos, comic strips, and video games are all examples of media that entertain. They make us laugh, sing, watch, or play.

Target Audience

The purpose, form, and target audience of a media text are interrelated. Every media text is created for one or more purposes and with some type of audience in mind. The target audience might be general (such as any adult), or specific (such as children between ages 8 and 12 who have a specific interest).

A form is chosen to suit the purpose, but the target audience may also influence the choice of form. For example, forms that rely mainly on visuals are more appropriate for a target audience of young children than forms that rely mainly on text. The audience affects the purpose, because the purpose must be appropriate for the intended audience.

Deconstructing Media Texts

To fully understand what a media text communicates, students need to be able to interpret both clear messages (messages clearly stated in the text) and hidden messages (messages that are implied). Students also need to be able to identify values (beliefs about what is important in life) that are communicated in a media text and to decide whether they share those values. By becoming aware of the persuasive techniques used in media texts, students learn to see how some media texts seek to manipulate their audience.

Examining Media—Activity Ideas

Identifying the Purpose(s) of Media Texts

1. Explain to students that every person who creates a media text has a reason for creating it. The reason for creating something is its *purpose*. Explain to students that there are three main purposes for creating media texts.

   • Some people who create media texts want to give you information or ideas. Their purpose is to *inform*.

   • Some people who create media texts want to give you enjoyment. They might want you to laugh or enter an imaginary world in books or movies. Their purpose is to *entertain*.

   • Some people who create media texts want you to believe something, buy something, or do something. Their purpose is to *persuade*.

2. As a class, examine various media texts one at a time and ask students why they think the item was created. Be sure to ask students to use the clues in the media text to explain the reasoning for their choice.

3. To reinforce the idea that every media text has a purpose or purposes, have students complete the various blackline masters provided as appropriate for their grade level.

Class Media Purpose Chart

Create a class chart, using the headings "Inform," "Entertain," and "Persuade" (or use other headings of your choice). As various media texts are introduced, have students decide where each one should be categorized. Students should soon realize that some media texts have more than one purpose. For example, a DVD about baby animals can inform and entertain.

Introducing the World of Advertising

1. Ask students, "What is an advertisement or ad?" Discuss with students how advertisements try to convince people to buy something, do something, or believe in something. Brainstorm places where students see advertisements, such as in magazines, ads, billboards, product packaging, logos, commercials, etc.

2. Next show students some examples of print advertisements. For each advertisement, ask the following:

   • Who made this advertisement?

   • What is this advertisement trying to make you think? What are the clues?

   • How do the advertisers try to grab your attention with pictures, colors, etc.?

   • What words or phrases are they using to make you want to buy this product?

3. Create a chart of words and phrases that advertisers may use to convince someone to buy their product. These may include words such as "amazing" and "incredible," and phrases such as, "Buy now before it is too late" or "The only choice."

4. Explore the concept of advertising further by completing **BLM 20: What Is Advertising?**

Exploring Persuasive Techniques in Advertising

As you introduce various commercials and print advertisements, explore with students the ways advertisers try to convince people to buy their product. These techniques may include

- repeated words
- catchy song
- prizes
- showing kids having fun
- characters kids know
- catchy phrases
- repeated words
- discounts
- music

On chart paper, keep track of persuasive techniques so students may refer to them when they create their own advertisements. The list below are words and phrases commonly found in advertising.

- Amazing
- Announcing
- At last!
- Before it is too late!
- Just arrived
- Last chance!
- Be the first!
- Introducing
- New and improved!
- First choice!
- Easy
- Recommended by
- Quick
- Hurry
- New
- Free

Also have students complete **BLM 21: Convincing People to Buy a Product** to gain more of an understanding.

What Is a Commercial?

It is important to teach and reinforce with younger students the difference between a television program and a commercial. One way to do this is to use a timer when viewing a commercial with students to show when it begins and ends. A commercial is very short. A television program is long. Point out that the purpose of the commercial is to sell a product. The purpose of a television program is usually to entertain or to inform.

- What are some examples of commercials you have seen on television?
- Did those ads make you want to buy the product? Explain why or why not.
- When you want to buy something, what are some things should you think about first?

Decoding Commercials

1. Have on hand recorded television commercials aimed at children the age of your students. One commercial should have a jingle or repeated slogan. As a class, view one of the commercials.

2. To get students to start questioning what they are watching on an ongoing basis, use the following sample questions as discussion starters:

   • What is the commercial trying to tell us?
   • Do you believe its message? Why or why not?
   • Who is the target audience for this commercial? How do you know?
   • How does this commercial make you feel? Explain why.
   • What things in the commercial grabbed your attention and made you want to watch it?
   • Would your family like to watch this commercial? Why or why not?
   • What information is missing from the message?
   • Who do you think paid for this commercial to be made? Explain your thinking.

3. Sample discussion starters specific to toy commercials include

   • Who makes toy commercials?
   • What happens in the commercial that might make kids want to buy that toy?
   • Which television toy commercials do you like to watch? Why?
   • Which television toy commercials do you not like to watch? Why?
   • Why do you think some toys are based on children's movies and television shows?

Jingles and Slogans

1. Explain to students that *jingles* are short catchy songs that are easy to remember, and *slogans* are words or phrases that are easy to remember. Companies create jingles and slogans to help people remember their products. Write a few examples of jingles and slogans on the board and ask students to identify the product associated with each.

2. Talk about why jingles and slogans work. Ask students why they think people remember jingles and slogans. For example, they are short, easy to remember, repeated several times, they stick in your mind, and the music is catchy.

3. Ask students to identify a few of their favorite jingles and slogans, and to explain why they like them.

4. Have students create a jingle or a slogan for something, such as about being in grade _____, a new product, or their favorite _____. When students are creating their jingles, suggest that they base it on a song they are familiar with such as "Twinkle, Twinkle, Little Star."

Finding Clear and Hidden Messages

1. Recall with students that all media texts have messages. Explain that they often have two messages—one that is very clear and one that is hidden.

2. Show students samples of media texts. For each sample, talk about the clear and hidden messages. Ask students how they feel about these messages. Use questions to guide their understanding. For example, for a cartoon that has humor mixed with violence, ask,

   • What is funny about this cartoon?
   • What message does this give you about violence?
   • Is violence a good way to solve problems? Why or why not?
   • Do you like this cartoon? Why or why not?
   • Who might like this cartoon? Who might not like this cartoon?

   For a print advertisement showing two boys playing with a toy car or a game, ask,

   • What is happening in this ad?
   • How are the boys feeling? How do you know?
   • What message does this give you?
   • The ad shows boys playing. Is there a hidden message about who the toy is for?
   • Would you like to play with this toy? Why or why not?

3. Students can use **BLM 23: Media Messages** to further explore clear and hidden media messages. Have students answer the questions, then discuss their responses as a class.

Identifying Facts and Opinions

1. Discuss with students the difference between a fact (information that is generally known to be true or has been proven to be true) and an opinion (a personal view or judgment which may or may not be based on facts). Point out that sometimes opinions are easy to identify because they contain words such as "I think," "I believe," and "in my opinion."

2. Explain that people sometimes state opinions as though they were facts; for example, "Spring is the best season of the year." Present students with some statements and ask them to decide which are facts and which are opinions. Possible examples include the following:

   • Dogs make better pets than cats. (opinion)
   • In the United States, summer is the warmest season of the year. (fact)
   • Spaghetti is the best dinner. (opinion)
   • On most television stations, shows have commercials. (fact)

3. Provide opportunities for students to distinguish between facts and opinions within a variety of media texts such as non-fiction books and print advertisements. Use **BLM 24: Fact or Opinion?** to organize findings.

Examining Point of View in Media Texts

1. Ask students what they know about the story of the three little pigs. Read the traditional version aloud.

   Note: Many traditional versions of this story have the first two pigs eaten by the wolf, and the wolf boiled by the third pig. To fit better with the role-play activity (see step 4 below), you may wish to read a version in which neither the pigs nor the wolf die.

2. Ask students who the main characters are in the story. Guide students to understand that the story is told from the pigs' point of view. The story is about what happened to them— why they left home, why they build the houses they did, and how the last pig tricked the wolf. The story is written as though the pigs are telling the story.

3. Tell students that you are going to read a different version of the story. In this version, the wolf tells the story from his point of view. Read *The True Story of the 3 Little Pigs!* aloud. Discuss the differences in the story. Talk about how the wolf's view of what happened is different from the pigs' point of view in the traditional version.

4. Choose another fairy tale, such as *Jack and the Beanstalk*, to discuss different points of view. Briefly summarize the story for students. Then ask students to think about how the giant felt about what happened. Ask how they would feel if someone came into their home and stole something that was very important to them. Ask students to imagine that the giant was telling the story. Discuss what he might say. For example, prompt students with sentence starters such as

   I was sitting at my table eating _____.
   I asked my wife to bring me _____.
   The next thing I knew, a boy _____.
   I ran after him, but _____.
   Now I have no money because _____.

Role-playing the Stories

1. Arrange students into groups of four. Assign either *The Three Little Pigs* or *The True Story of the 3 Little Pigs!* to each group. Within each group, assign (or have students choose) one of the roles: Pig 1, Pig 2, Pig 3, or the Wolf.

2. Tell students that you are going to role-play a news reporter who will interview each group about the events of the day. Students will role-play their characters and answer questions. Allow time for students to think about what their characters might say about what happened and how they felt, then interview each group.

Imagination: Amazing Stories

Media texts such as movies, books, and television shows are often ways for people to escape to another world—a world in which people and animals can do things and be things that are not possible in real life. In some media texts, animals can talk and do other things humans can do, and people can do superhuman things such as fly and walk through walls. Use **BLM 25: Amazing Stories** to explore how imagination is used to create stories.

Distinguishing Between Real Life and Media Texts

Ideas for movies, books, and television shows come from the writers' imagination, but they also come from real life. Often, real-life situations are exaggerated in media texts to make them funny or unrealistic. For example, some people can jump very high in real life. But, in a movie, the writer might exaggerate that ability so the person jumps to the top of a building. Students should be able to distinguish between things that can happen and things that cannot happen in real life. Students can use **BLM 26: Real or Not?** to analyze how realistic a story, television show, or movie is. Have students share their findings, and discuss as a class.

• Could this story happen in real life? Explain your thinking.
• In what ways is it like real life? In what ways is not like real life?
• How do the author and illustrator make the story and pictures seem real?
• How does the moviemaker make the story seem real?
• Do you like this book, movie, or television show? Why or why not?
• Do you think all people will have the same opinion? Why or why not?

Thinking About Target Audience

1. Discuss with students how every media text is created with a specific audience in mind, and that this audience may be large or small. For example, a telephone directory is created for a very large audience (anyone who uses a phone). But when a student writes a sticky note that says "Remember gym is on Thursday," this media text has a very small audience. It is just for the person who wrote the note.

2. Ask students general questions about books they like. For example,

   • What is your favorite picture book?
   • Who else do you think might like to read this book?
   • Who do you think might not like to read this book?
   • Who do you think this book was made for?

   Continue with other examples such as print advertisements, television shows, computer games, and websites. Then explain to students that media texts or products such as these are made for a target audience—the group of people who would like it, and will buy or use it.

A Cereal for Who?

1. Show students the children's cereal box(es). Allow them to examine the box. Ask them to describe what they see on the box. List their responses on the board. Guide them to consider such things as the name of the cereal, familiar characters, games, color, type of lettering used, words or phrases, and nutritional content (what the cereal is made from).

2. Show them the adult cereal box(es) and repeat.

3. Read over the lists with students. Ask them what is the same and what is different about each of the boxes. For example, they may note that the children's cereal has a character they know from television or books. The adult cereal may instead show a real person doing something healthy. Both cereal boxes show the nutritional content. The children's cereal box may contain a toy or game, but the adult cereal box does not.

4. Review the words and phrases used on both types of boxes. Discuss as a class these words and phrases, noting fun words used such as "deee-licious!" or "crrrrunchy!" and more serious words such as "healthy" and "whole grain."

5. Discuss with students why each of the boxes would appeal to the audience it was made for.

6. As a follow-up activity, have students fold a large piece of paper in half. On one half of the paper, have students create an advertisement for a product or service directed at children. On the other half, have students create an advertisement for the same product or service but directed at adults. When students are finished, ask them to share their reasoning for the different persuasive techniques they used for each of their advertisements.

Favorite Characters

1. Ask students who their favorite characters are from books, television shows (including cartoons), and movies. Make a list on the board. Talk about why these characters are their favorites, using questions such as

- What do you like about the character?
- How does the character act? How does the character talk? How do they dress?
- What message do you get from the character? What is the character telling you about how to behave?
- Do you want to be like this character? Why or why not?

2. Provide students with **BLM 27: My Favorite Character**. Have students draw the character doing something that shows why they like that character. Ask students to complete the sentence to explain what they like or admire most about the character. Encourage students to write more than one sentence if they can.

What Is a Purpose?

A purpose is the reason why we do something. Just about everything you do has a purpose. Here are some examples.

What You Do		Your Purpose
Put on a sweater		To stay warm
Water a plant		To help the plant grow
Go to school		To learn
Go to sleep		To rest
Play with toys		To have fun

Think About It!

What Is a Purpose?

Think about two things you do in a day and explain the purpose for each.

What I Do	What is the purpose?

BLM 16

Media Purposes

People create media for different reasons or purposes. The different types of media we see and hear have different purposes.

What are some of the purposes of different forms of media? Look at the chart below.

Media Form		Purpose
Television commercial		To convince people to buy something
Picture book		To let people have fun reading the story and looking at the pictures
Television news show		To give people information about what is happening in the world

Media Purposes

1. Chris watches a commercial about a new robot toy. What is the purpose of the commercial?

_____

2. Sophia reads a recipe to make a cake. What is the purpose of the recipe?

_____

continued next page ☞

BLM 17

3. Some media forms have the purpose of giving people information.

Some media forms have the purpose of letting people have fun.

Use a check mark to show the purpose of each media form below.

Media Form	What is the purpose?
a) Comic book	☐ Give information ☐ Let people have fun
b) Newspaper	☐ Give information ☐ Let people have fun
c) Radio weather report	☐ Give information ☐ Let people have fun
d) Movie	☐ Give information ☐ Let people have fun
e) Television game show	☐ Give information ☐ Let people have fun
f) Map	☐ Give information ☐ Let people have fun
g) Menu	☐ Give information ☐ Let people have fun
h) Song	☐ Give information ☐ Let people have fun

What Is the Purpose?

1. Read the descriptions of the media examples.

2. For each media example, use a check mark to show its purpose.

Media Example	Purpose
a) A recipe for cookies	☐ Inform ☐ Persuade ☐ Entertain
b) A cartoon	☐ Inform ☐ Persuade ☐ Entertain
c) A report in the newspaper about a hockey game	☐ Inform ☐ Persuade ☐ Entertain
d) An advertisement about a new type of running shoe	☐ Inform ☐ Persuade ☐ Entertain
e) A television commercial about a new movie	☐ Inform ☐ Persuade ☐ Entertain
f) A video game about a frog	☐ Inform ☐ Persuade ☐ Entertain

BLM 18

Media—What Is the Purpose?

- Draw a **$** if the person who created the media text wants you to buy something.

- Draw a **?** if the person who created the media text wants to tell you something.

- Draw a ☺ if the person who created the media text wants you to have fun.

_____

_____

_____

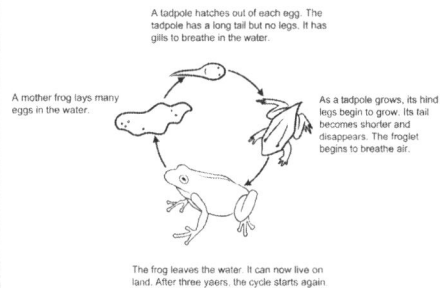

_____

What Is Advertising?

Companies make products, such as running shoes, breakfast cereals, and toys. Companies sell products to make money.

To sell a product, companies send out messages to tell people about the product. Telling people about a product is called *advertising*.

Different Forms of Advertising

You have seen and heard commercials on television and on the radio. Commercials are a form of advertising. Here are some other forms of advertising:

• Magazine ads   • Billboards   • Packages that products come in

The Purposes of Advertising

Companies advertise products for two reasons:

• To let people know about the product they are selling
• To make people want to buy the product

Lots of companies make the same type of product. For example, Henry's Soup Company makes vegetable soup. The Tasty Soup Company also makes vegetable soup. Each company wants you to buy their vegetable soup instead of the vegetable soup the other company makes. So each company will use advertising to help sell their soup. Each company's advertising will try to convince you that their soup is better than the soup the other company makes.

What Is Advertising?

Think about products that you have seen advertised. Choose one food product and one toy or game. Then answer the questions below.

Food Product

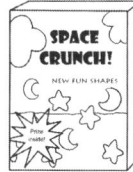

1. What food product did you choose?

_____

2. What form of advertising told you about this product?

_____

3. Did the advertising make you want to buy the product? Tell why or why not.

_____

_____

Toy or Game

4. What toy or game did you choose?

_____

5. What form of advertising told you about this product?

_____

6. Did the advertising make you want to buy the product? Tell why or why not.

_____

_____

Convincing People to Buy a Product

Advertising tries to convince people to buy the product that is advertised. What are some ways that advertising tries to do this?

Give Facts About the Product

A fact is a piece of information that is always true. Here is an example of a fact: *Yummy Crunch cereal is made from wheat.* The company that makes this cereal can prove that it is always made from wheat. This is a fact because it is always true.

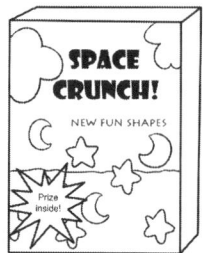

Give Opinions About the Product

An opinion is a piece of information that is true for some people, but not for everyone. Here is an example of an opinion: *Yummy Crunch is the best cereal I have ever tasted.* Some people might agree that Yummy Crunch is the best cereal they have ever tasted. Other people might think that another type of cereal tastes better. The opinion that Yummy Crunch tastes best is not true for everyone.

Compare the Product to Similar Products

Imagine that you have created a new cereal called Tasty Bites. You want to convince people to buy your cereal instead of Yummy Crunch. Your advertising could compare Tasty Bites to Yummy Crunch. Here are two examples:

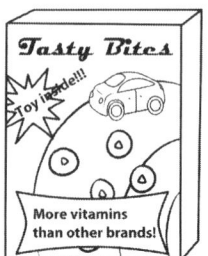

• Tasty Bites has more vitamins than Yummy Crunch.

• Tasty Bites has a toy inside but Yummy Crunch does not.

BLM 21

Convincing People to Buy a Product

1. Read the sentences you might see in advertising. Put a check mark beside each sentence to tell whether it is a fact or an opinion.

Statement	Fact or opinion?
a) Super Fast running shoes come in four different colors.	☐ Fact ☐ Opinion
b) You will love your new Super Fast running shoes.	☐ Fact ☐ Opinion
c) Your whole family will enjoy playing the Race to Win board game.	☐ Fact ☐ Opinion
d) Race to Win comes with four game pieces and two dice.	☐ Fact ☐ Opinion

2. Think of a product that you or your family have bought. Give one fact and one opinion about the product.

Name of product: _____

A fact about the product: _____

_____

_____

An opinion about the product: _____

_____

_____

continued next page ☞

3. What is your favorite food? _____

Create a food character. Give it a name. _____

Draw a picture of your food character with your favorite food. Add some words to make an ad.

4. In what ways does your ad make children want to try your favorite food? _____

_____

_____

Media Detective

Look at an advertisement or view a commercial. Answer these questions.

Media message: _____

What is the message?	What are the clues?

Who made the message?	What are the clues?

Who is the target audience for the message?	What are the clues?

How does the message try to convince the target audience?	What are the clues?

Media Messages

Clear Messages

The media we see send us messages that are clear. A picture book tells us what happens to the characters in the story. A commercial tells us about a new product people can buy. These messages are easy to understand because the words give us the message.

Messages That Are Not Clear

Sometimes media send us messages that are not clear because the message is not in words. Let us look at an example.

Imagine there is a commercial for a new board game. The words in the commercial tell what the game is called and how to play it. Those are clear messages.

The commercial shows video of a group of children playing the game. The children are all laughing and having fun. This part of the commercial sends the message, "If you get this game, you will have as much fun playing it as the children in the commercial." The commercial does not give this message in words. The video of the children having fun sends us this message.

Media sometimes send us messages that are not clear because the message is not in words.

Media Messages

1. Think about the game commercial described in "Media Messages." Imagine that the commercial showed a video of children looking bored as they played the game. What message would this send?

_____

_____

_____

2. Imagine the game commercial showed adults playing the game. What message would this send about who the target audience is for this game?

_____

_____

_____

3. The game commercial shows children having fun playing the game. Does this mean that everyone will enjoy playing the game? Why or why not?

_____

_____

_____

_____

_____

Fact or Opinion?

Media text: _____

Purpose of media text: _____

Short description of media text: _____

_____

Look for examples of facts and opinions in the media text you are examining.

Fact	Opinion

Amazing Stories

What Is Real in Stories?

Books are not the only place where we find stories. Movies and television shows tell stories too. Amazing things happen in many stories.

Sometimes stories tell us about things that could really happen. You might read a story about a girl who finds a buried treasure. That could really happen. Sometimes people really do find buried treasure.

You might also see a movie about a boy who can make himself invisible. In real life, people cannot make themselves invisible. Sometimes things happen in stories that cannot happen in real life.

Use Your Imagination

People use their imagination to create interesting stories. You could write a story about a place where all the trees are blue. There is no such place in real life, but it might be fun to write a story about it.

You could write a story about strange monsters with purple fur. In real life, there are no monsters with purple fur. When you write a story, you can use your imagination to write about things that are not real.

People use their imagination to create the stories we see in books, television shows, and movies. Some stories are about things that are not real. In a story, anything can happen!

1. In a fairy tale, a boy plants a seed. The seed grows into a plant that is so tall it touches the sky.

   Put a **check mark** beside the things that could happen in real life.
   Put an **X** beside things that could not happen in real life.

   _____ **A boy plants a seed.**

   _____ **The seed grows into a plant.**

   _____ **The plant grows so tall that it touches the sky.**

2. On a television show, a girl gets a toy robot for her birthday. She gets the robot to do her homework for her. Then her cat climbs onto her desk. The cat says, "You should not let the robot do your homework for you!"

   a) Write two things from the television show that could really happen.

   _____

   _____

   _____

   _____

   b) Write two things from the television show that could not really happen.

   _____

   _____

   _____

   _____

Real or Not?

Read or listen to a story, or watch a movie or television show. Write which things could happen in real life, and which things could not.

1. I am writing about

☐ a story I read or listened to   ☐ a television show   ☐ a movie

Title: _____

a) Things that could happen in real life:

_____

_____

_____

_____

b) Things that could not happen in real life:

_____

_____

_____

_____

_____

My Favorite Character

1. Draw your favorite character below.

2. Show the character doing something you like.

3. Complete the sentence below.

_____ is my favorite character

because _____

_____

_____

BLM 27

Creating Media Texts

Background Information

The purpose of media literacy education is to encourage students to become critical "consumers" of media. It helps them learn to discriminate facts from opinions, interpret clear and hidden messages, understand the values presented in a media texts, and identify any persuasive techniques that are used. However, students also need to learn how to create effective media texts. Analyzing and creating media texts are activities that reinforce each other. Students can apply what they learn from analyzing media texts to creating their own media texts. By creating media texts, students will learn what types of decisions need to be made and make those decisions themselves based on the purpose, form, and target audience. As a result, students improve their ability to deconstruct the media texts they read, view, and listen to.

Listening to a Media Expert

Invite into the classroom someone whose profession involves creating media texts. For example, invite a reporter from a local newspaper or television station, a graphic artist, a Web designer, or someone from an advertising agency. Ask the guest to share with students details about their job and, if possible, to share some media texts they were involved in creating. (You might first brief the guest on what students have been learning about media and ask them to touch on some these topics during the presentation.) Provide time for students to ask questions.

Teacher Tips for Creating Media Text Activities

- Model and reinforce required skills. If students are not familiar with the characteristics and conventions of a type of media text, they will have a difficult time using it to create an effective product.
- Make sure there are enough materials for each student, along with a sample of what is expected.
- Have students create media portfolios where they can store their media projects, assignments, and learning logs.

Creating Media Texts—Activity Ideas

Exploring Creating Media

To help students create the following media texts, have them read and complete **BLM 28: Creating Media**. This should give students a good base on which to build their ideas.

Class Newsletter

Keep parents informed about class activities with this easy weekly newsletter! Students can use **BLM 34: Our Class Newsletter** to create a one-page newsletter of all the things they do in class over the course of one week. Students can use drawings, words, cutout pictures, or any combination to create their newsletter. When students are finished, they can share their newsletters with the class. Encourage students to take their newsletters home to share with their family or caregiver.

For younger students, take a few minutes at the end of each school day to ask students what they learned in school. Record each comment in the appropriate day of the week. You may wish to also record a student's initials after each comment. Use the notes box to recommend a website or to remind parents about important information.

Personal Bookmark

Students can create a fun, themed bookmark using **BLM 35: Create Your Own Bookmark**. Bookmark subjects should be something the student is interested in such as a hobby, favorite subject, or class theme. Have students write, draw, or glue pictures on the front and back of their bookmark. Some students may prefer to write a favorite saying or a few words on their bookmark, or use a combination of pictures and words. Then have students carefully cut out the bookmark, fold it in half lengthwise, then glue it together.

Friend T-shirt

Brainstorm with students what it means to be a good friend to someone. Ask, "What types of things make a person a good friend to you? What does a good friend do? What does a good friend say? How does a good friend act?" Students can create a T-shirt using **BLM 36: Design a Friend T-shirt** to show tips on how to be a good friend to someone. Students can design their T-shirt using just words, or they can include drawings or cutout pictures. Display students' finished T-shirts around the classroom and hold a gallery walk to view their creations.

Retell a Story

Inform students that they will be retelling a story in their own words. Ask students to choose a favorite story, or a story they have recently read as a class. Recall with students that every story has a beginning, a middle, and an ending. Have students use **BLM 37: Super Story Retell** to guide their writing. Alternatively, you may wish to assign students to retell a story from different points of view then compare versions as a class.

Personal Flag

Have students create a flag that is unique to them using **BLM 40: My Own Personal Flag**. It can show something they are interested in, or something about their family heritage. Encourage students to create a unique flag. Provide students with drawing materials to use to create their flag.

Story-Writing Workshop

Students can write a story, using **BLM 41: Story-Writing Workshop** as an outline to guide their writing. When students are finished, provide them with choices such as using a computer program to publish their story and illustrating it in a particular style.

Acrostic Poems

Describe to students the conventions of an acrostic poem. A name or word is written vertically, with one letter on each line. Each letter is then used to start a short sentence or a word that describes, or is related in some way to, the original name or word. For example,

S - is for my sister Sarah
A - is for always laughing with me
R - is for her red, wavy hair
A - is for the art she draws so well

Bicycles are fun
In spring and summer
Kids ride bikes
Everywhere

Students can use **BLM 42: Acrostic Poem** to create their poem.

Personal Postcard

Students can use **BLM 43: Personal Postcard** to create postcards from real or imaginary places.

Wanted!

Have students create a wanted poster for a character from a book or television program. Students can use **BLM 44: Wanted Poster** as a form to create their poster. Encourage them to use attention-grabbing words, such as fastest, slowest, strongest, meanest, craziest, or loudest, to describe the character and why they are wanted. Remind them to include a reward for capture. Students could also include where the character was last seen.

Communicating Directions

Give students an opportunity to explain how to do something or how to go somewhere. Emphasize to students that they need to think carefully about the order when writing out directions.

1. What happens first?
2. What happens next (second)?
3. What happens next (third)?
4. What happens last?

Reinforce vocabulary that will help others to understand their directions. For example,

• Order words: first, second, last, next, after, before
• Direction words: right, left, forward, behind
• Procedure words: turn, put, hold, spin, stop

Complete a few examples as a class, then have students write their own directions or procedure.

Review a Book, Play, or Movie

Have students write their own review of a book, play, or movie. Students can use **BLM 45: Write a Review** to guide their writing.

Special Stamp

Students can create their own personal stamp using **BLM 46: Special Stamp**. Brainstorm things and people they have seen on stamps. Ask students why these people and things might have been presented in that form. Recall with students that subjects on stamps include famous Canadians, provincial plants and animals, endangered species, and events (Olympics). Then students can create their own stamp to send out the message of what is important to them.

Student of the Week

Having a Student of the Week is a great way to promote self-esteem and instill pride in students. It will also encourage students to learn more about their classmates and will send the message that they are all part of the class community. At the beginning of the school year, have families choose the week that their child will be Student of the Week. In preparation for that week, ask families to send in special photographs of the student to display (such as baby photos), and a bag of items that the student would like to share and display. Create a bulletin board display of the student's information, pictures, and school work. You may also wish to include written notes from classmates that compliment or recognize the student chosen to be Student of the Week.

A Picture Is...

Ask students to paint a picture or snap a photograph of something in their neighborhood. Ask them to give it a catchy headline, along with a cutline to describe what is happening in the picture. Visual elements such as photographs and illustrations are key elements used in newspapers and magazines. As an alternative, have students choose a picture from a magazine or newspaper.

Build a Class Website

Investing the time to create a class website is definitely worthwhile. Use the website as a springboard for all the wonderful things happening in your classroom.

Class Big Book

As a class, publish a big book. Assign one page of the class big book to each student or have students work in small cooperative groups. The complexity of the class big book will be dependent on students' abilities. Younger students can print a missing word to complete a sentence, and create an illustration for a page. Older students could create drafts first, then plan how to layout their page. You may wish to allow students to take the big book home for a night to share with their family.

Ideas for a class big book include

• Spinoff version of a favorite class book with repetitive text
• ABC book based on a theme
• Recalling class field trips
• A collection of nonfiction reports based on a topic studied
• A list of favorite _____
• Retelling of a story and imitating the style of the illustrator
• Retelling a story based on a different character's point of view

Restaurant Menu

Have students examine several examples of menus from a variety of restaurants. Brainstorm a list of characteristics that can be seen in most menus. Discuss the persuasive language and visual elements that make menus appealing. Then have students create their own restaurant menus with a target audience in mind.

Oral Presentation

Have students use **BLM 47: Oral Presentation Outline** to prepare for a public speaking activity, or as a response to something they have viewed or read.

Class Audio Book

As a class, or in small groups, record an audio version of a picture book. Cast students in roles, and insert sound effects and music to accentuate dramatic or pivotal moments in the story. Ask students to identify the main message in the book and how the message translates in this new format.

Teacher Prompts

• Do we interpret media messages differently when we listen than we do when we read?
• Is the message the same in both media forms?
• Did you pick up new details in the text or messages by creating the audio version?
• What parts worked better as a book?
• What parts worked better as an audio book?
• How does bringing dialogue to life change the book?

Greeting Card

Brainstorm with students a list of reasons why people give greeting cards. Then have students decide on a message for their card and create it. Encourage students to convey their message through a riddle, poetry, or the use of humor.

Dear _____ :

Some newspapers and magazines contain advice columns where people can write in to ask for advice about a problem or situation they are facing. Brainstorm with students some situations for which people might ask for advice. Have students choose from the list or think of another topic, and use **BLM 48: A Letter of Advice** to write their letter. You may wish to invite students to share their letters with the class.

Be Proud!

Every person has reasons to be proud of themselves. Have students write ten reasons they are proud on **BLM 49: I Am Proud to Be Me!** Encourage students to use complete sentences when writing their reasons.

Signs and Symbols

Review with students how it is possible to communicate a message without using words. Brainstorm a list of examples such as signs or symbols in your community. Then challenge students to create their own signs or symbols to communicate a specific message.

Draw a Map

Maps serve many purposes. Maps can show the location of towns, cities, provinces, countries, and continents. Maps can also show the location of places inside buildings, malls, zoos, and amusement parks. Maps can even show imaginary places or the location of a pirate treasure! Have students use **BLM 50: My Marvelous Map**. Students can draw a map showing the items in their bedroom, their classroom, playground, or a make-believe pirate treasure on an island. Maps can be simple or detailed, according to students' abilities. Remind students to include a legend.

Design a Poster

Posters advertise many things, such as school events, concerts, CDs, movies, television shows, clothing, perfume, beauty products, foods, drinks, stores, vehicles, and vacation destinations. They also advertise upcoming events. Have students create a poster to advertise something from the above list, or of their own choosing. Remind them to use persuasive words and phrases. Students can use **BLM 51: Poster Checklist** to help them create an interesting, persuasive, and eye-catching poster.

Create a Board Game

Have students work in groups to develop an idea for a new board game. Students can use **BLM 52: Create a Board Game** for ideas and steps to follow to create their game. Students can invite another group to play their finished game.

Breaking News!

Have students choose a favorite book or story they have heard or read. Ask them to use **BLM 53: News Story** to create a short news story about a character or an event from the story. Remind them to use attention-grabbing words to make people want to read the story. Students may also wish to write a news story based on real life, such as a class event or field trip.

Create a Character Collage

Have students choose a character from a favorite book or story. Students can create a collage about the character using pictures and words from magazines, brochures, or newspapers. Students can cut and paste the pictures and words onto a piece of paper. Display students' collages around the classroom and hold a gallery walk to view them.

Pantomime

Pantomime is a great activity to teach students how to act out a story without using words. Explain to students that they are only allowed to use hand gestures, facial expressions, and body movements to communicate a particular action from the story. In a whole-group setting, give students a variety of actions so they can practice pantomime. For example, have them act out eating something tasty, then eating something horrible, brushing their teeth, acting surprised, and imitating people or animals doing various activities.

Cinquain Poem

A cinquain poem has five lines and describes a person, place, or thing.

The poem has a pattern, but does not have to rhyme. Show students examples of cinquains to help them become familiar with the form.

Dog	a one-word title, a noun
brown, furry	two adjectives
barking, running, jumping	three *-ing* participles
having fun	a phrase
pet	a synonym for your title, another noun

Sales Pitch

Have students present a sales pitch about a product or about a book they have read. The rest of the class could pretend they are clerks in a store. Encourage students to use persuasive language and gimmicks to entice the audience.

Drama Center

A drama center promotes students' practice of language skills through the communication of ideas and dramatic play. Set up a drama center to represent a specific place in your community. Encourage students to bring in items that can represent places in the community. For example,

• Post Office – provide items such as stamps, envelopes, stationary, a class mailbox, and assign a postal worker to deliver class mail
• Restaurant – provide a table, chairs, plastic cutlery, paper cups and plates, plastic food, and have students create a class café menu
• Radio Station – play microphone, a method of playing music

Creating Media

Here are some questions to think about when you create media.

What is my topic?

Make sure you understand what your topic is. Do not include information that is not really part of your topic.

What is my purpose?

Ask yourself, "Why am I creating this media?" Do you want to give people information or let them have fun when they see or hear your media? Do you want your media to convince people do something, such as buy a product?

Who is my target audience?

Ask yourself, "Who do I want to see or hear my media?" Is it for everyone, or is it for a smaller group? Is for adults, or for children? Is it mostly for boys, or mostly for girls? Is it just for family and friends?

What media form should I choose?

Sometimes your teacher may ask you to use a certain media form, such as a poster, a story, a collage, or a magazine ad to sell a product. If you can choose what media form you want to use, think about these questions:

• What media form would work best for my purpose?
• What media form would work best for my target audience?

Creating Media

1. Pablo is creating a slideshow. His topic is "My Dog Sparky." Pablo has a great photograph of his pet goldfish. He wants to put the photograph in his slideshow too. Is this a good idea? Explain why or why not.

_____

_____

_____

_____

2. Julie is creating a poster. The title of her poster is "Play Safely on the Playground." Julie is not sure who her target audience is. Who would be a good target audience for Julie's poster? Explain why.

_____

_____

_____

_____

3. Sam wants to find a way to tell students to recycle paper. He might create a T-shirt he can wear that says, "Recycle some paper today!" Or he might create a brochure telling students why recycling paper is important. Which media form would be better? Explain why.

_____

_____

_____

_____

New and Improved Book Cover

Book Title: _____

Author: _____

Make up a new title for this book. Design a new book cover to go along with the book title.

My new book cover will get the attention of the reader by:

_____

Advertise a Teddy Bear!

Help design and complete the advertisement poster to encourage someone to buy this teddy bear.

Thinking About My Oral Report

My topic is _____

My Presentation	What I Think
• I began my oral report in an interesting way such as with a riddle or a question.	🙂 😐 🙁
• I used my best voice, spoke slowly, and made sure everyone could hear.	🙂 😐 🙁
• I really know about my topic and can answer questions.	🙂 😐 🙁
• My notes are organized.	🙂 😐 🙁
• I pointed to pictures, a model, or a diorama, as I presented.	🙂 😐 🙁

The best part of my presentation is _____

_____

I am proud of _____

I need to work on _____

Brilliant Brochure Checklist

A brochure is a folded booklet that gives descriptive information.
Use the checklist to plan your brochure.

Topic: _____

Step 1: Plan Your Brochure

❑ Take a piece of paper and fold the paper the
   same way your brochure will be folded.

❑ Print the heading for each section. Leave room
   underneath the heading to write some information
   and to place pictures.

Step 2: Rough Copy

❑ I checked the facts for each section of my brochure.

❑ I read my work to make sure it has all of the information.

❑ I added, deleted, or changed words to make my writing better.

Step 3: Final Editing Checklist

❑ I checked for spelling.

❑ My brochure is neat and easy to read.

❑ I checked for punctuation.

❑ My pictures go with the information.

❑ I checked for clear sentences.

❑ My brochure is attractive.

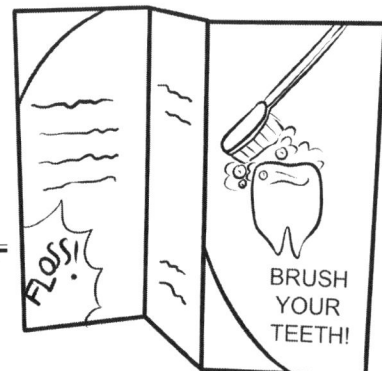

FLOSS!

BRUSH YOUR TEETH!

BLM 32

My Journal About...

☐ I checked for capitals and periods.

OUR CLASS NEWSLETTER

What did we do in school today?

MONDAY

TUESDAY

WEDNESDAY

THURSDAY

FRIDAY

NOTES

BLM 34

CREATE YOUR OWN BOOKMARK

Create a bookmark, cut it out, fold it in half, and glue it together!

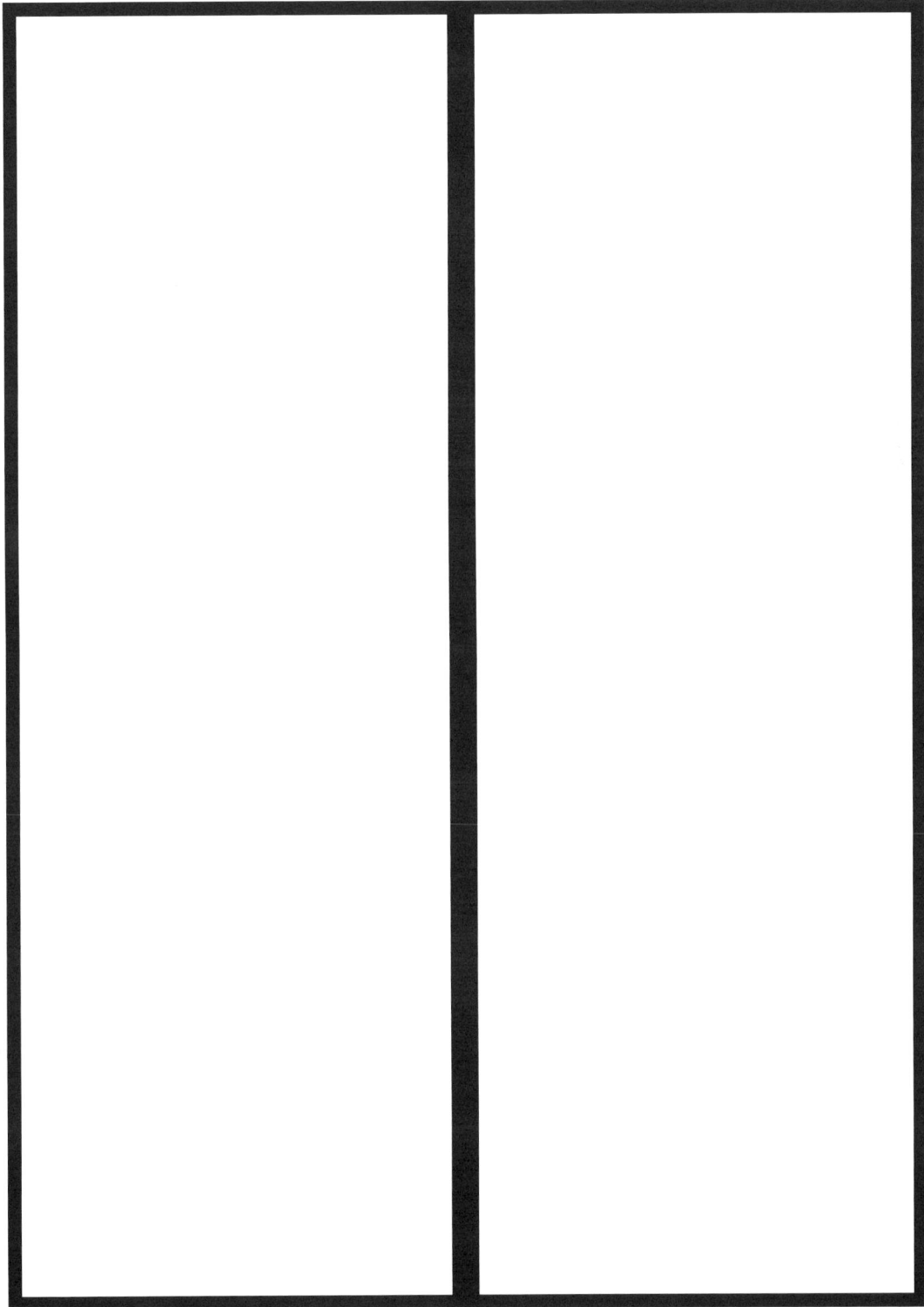

DESIGN A FRIEND T-SHIRT

Design a T-shirt that gives tips on how to be a good friend to someone.

BLM 36

SUPER STORY RETELL

Read a story. Retell what happened in the story in your own words.

Story Title: _____

BEGINNING:

_____

_____

_____

_____

_____

_____

continued next page ☞

BLM 37

MIDDLE:

_____

_____

_____

_____

_____

_____

_____

_____

_____

_____

continued next page ☞

BLM 37

ENDING:

_____

_____

_____

_____

_____

_____

_____

_____

My Favorite Part of the Story

Book Title: _____

This is a picture of my favorite part of the story.

What the story reminds me of:

_____

_____

BLM 38

Nonfiction Report

Topic: _____

Where did you find your information?

_____

What facts did you learn?

_____

_____

_____

_____

_____

_____

_____

_____

How will you present this information?

_____

My Own Personal Flag

Create your own personal flag. Make it colorful!

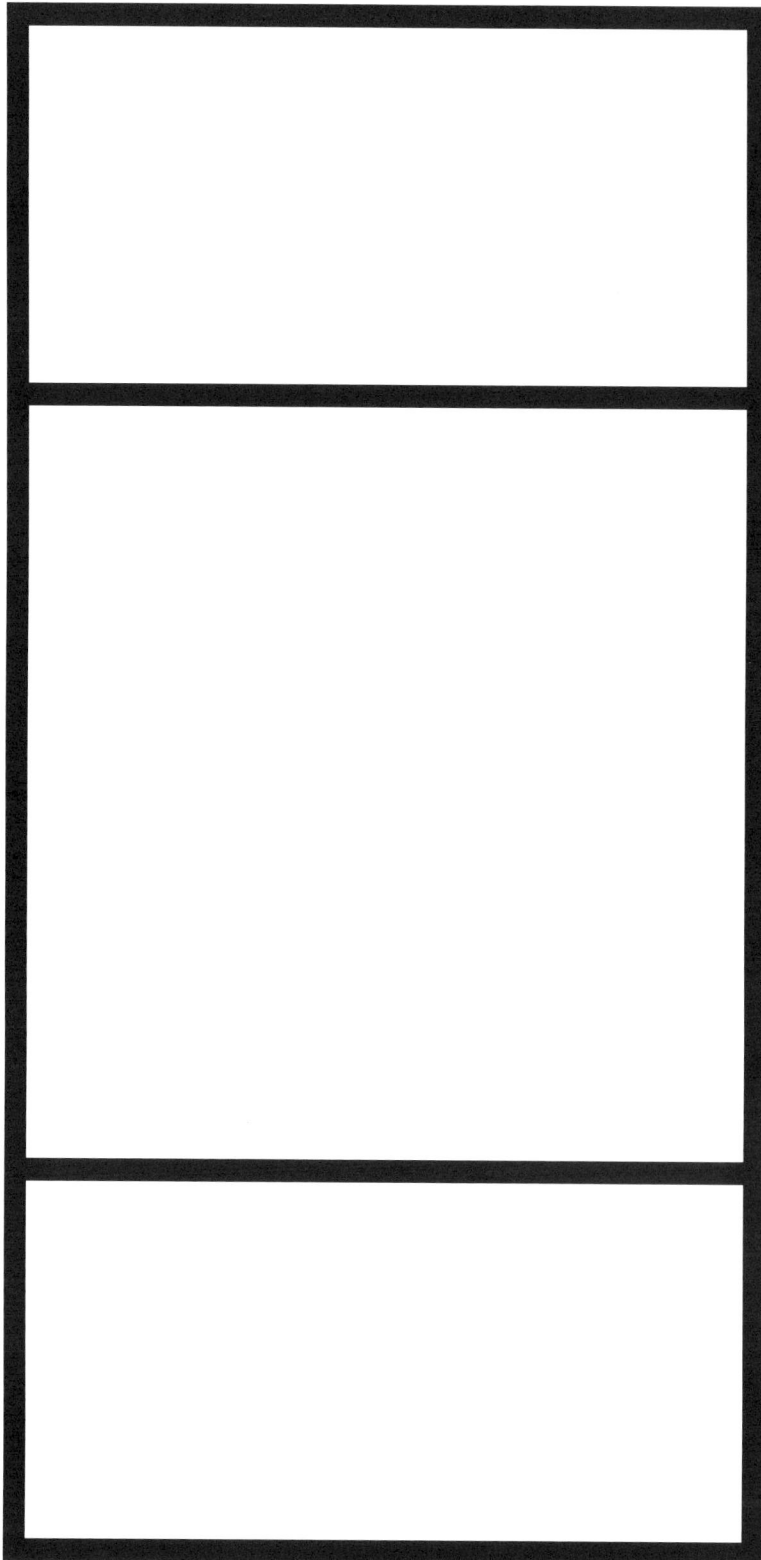

BLM 40

Story-Writing Workshop

Story Title: _____

BEGINNING:

- ☐ I wrote an attention-grabbing first sentence.
- ☐ I introduced the main character.
- ☐ I wrote about where the story takes place.

_____

_____

_____

_____

_____

_____

_____

_____

_____

☐ I checked for capitals and periods.   ☐ I added adjectives.

continued next page ☞

MIDDLE:

☐ **I explained the problem in the story.**

_____

_____

_____

_____

_____

_____

_____

_____

_____

_____

_____

_____

☐ **I checked for capitals and periods.**   ☐ **I added adjectives.**

continued next page ☞

BLM 41

EVENTS:

☐ I wrote about events that happen in the story before the problem is solved.

Event 1:

_____

_____

_____

_____

_____

Event 2:

_____

_____

_____

_____

_____

☐ I checked for capitals and periods.　　☐ I added adjectives.　　☐ I explained each event.

continued next page ☞

　　BLM 41

ENDING:

☐ I explained how the problem was solved.

_____

_____

_____

_____

_____

_____

_____

_____

_____

_____

_____

☐ I checked for capitals and periods.　　☐ I added adjectives.

ACROSTIC POEM

Acrostic poems are poems in which the first letter of each line forms a word or phrase (vertically). An acrostic poem can describe the subject or even tell a brief story about it.

Personal Postcard

Write a postcard to a friend.

Front of Postcard:

Back of Postcard:

To:

BLM 43

WANTED!

Name:

_____

Last seen:

_____

Description:

_____

_____

Wanted for:

_____

_____

Reward:

_____

BLM 44

Write a Review

Share your opinion about a book, play, or movie.

Title of Media: _____

Type of Media: _____

What was it about?

_____

_____

_____

In My Opinion:

_____

_____

_____

_____

_____

☐ Recommended

☐ Not recommended

Reviewed by:

_____

BLM 45

Special Stamp

Draw and color a special stamp.

Write about your stamp:

_____

_____

Oral Presentation Outline

Topic: _____

Target audience: _____

Purpose: _____

How long does it need to be? _____

Introduction Checklist

❏ I introduced my topic in an attention-grabbing way, such as
  ❏ a quote
  ❏ an example
  ❏ a question
❏ I state what I am going to talk about in 1 to 3 sentences.

continued next page ☞

BLM 47

Body Checklist

❑ My main idea has supporting details, examples, or descriptions.

❑ I wrote out my ideas the way I would sound if I were explaining, showing, or telling someone in person during a conversation.

❑ I read aloud what I wrote.

Tip: **You do not have to use full sentences. Write it the same way you talk.**

Main idea:

Supporting details:

continued next page ☞

BLM 47

Conclusion Checklist

❑ I summarized my key points.

❑ I ended my oral presentation in an attention-grabbing way, such as

    ❑ a quote

    ❑ a question

Presentation Delivery Tips

• Practice! Practice! Practice! Get comfortable with what you have written.

• Highlight your good copy in places where you would like to pause for effect, or emphasize a point.

• Think about hand gestures and making eye contact with the audience or camera.

• Think about your tone of voice to show enthusiasm.

BLM 47

A Letter of Advice

People ask for advice when they have a problem or would like an opinion about something. Give some advice to someone about a specific situation. Explain your thinking to convince the person that your advice is the right thing to do.

I am giving advice to _____

about _____

Dear _____,

_____

_____

_____

_____

_____

_____

_____

_____

Your friend,

_____

I Am Proud to Be Me!

List ten reasons why you are proud to be you.

1.	
2.	
3.	
4.	
5.	
6.	
7.	
8.	
9.	
10.	

BLM 49

My Marvelous Map

A map is a flat drawing of a place. Choose a place and draw a map. Create a legend that includes symbols to help people find things on your map.

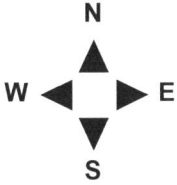

N

W ◄ ► E

S

LEGEND

Poster Checklist

Topic: _____

Purpose of Poster: _____

How does the poster look?	❏ The poster design is eye-catching. ❏ The heading gets the reader's attention.
Purpose and Content	❏ The message is clear. ❏ There are supporting facts, details, and/or descriptions.
Target Audience	❏ The target audience for the poster is clear.
Pictures	❏ The pictures help make the message of the poster clear. ❏ The pictures are colorful and look good.
Assigned Poster Requirements	❏ I completed all parts of the assignment.
Proofreading	❏ I checked the spelling. ❏ I checked the punctuation. ❏ I used attention-grabbing words and sentences.

I am proud of:

_____

Next time I will:

_____

BLM 51

Create a Board Game

Create your own board game! Base your game on a theme that you are studying in class or something that interests you.

WHAT YOU NEED

- A base for the game board, such as a large piece of construction paper, a clean takeout pizza box, or file folder
- Coloring materials
- Scissors
- Glue
- Construction paper
- 2 number cubes

WHAT YOU DO

1. Choose a theme for your game.
2. Create a path the game pieces will follow. You may choose to give your path a specific shape: a U-shape, an L-shape, a square, or an oval. Make your path at least 50 squares long.
3. Add spaces where you have to stack question cards cut from heavy paper. Print or handwrite questions on the cards.
4. Test the game to see if it is too hard or has enough spaces.
5. Cut small figures out of paper to use as game pieces, or use materials that are available.
6. Decorate your game board to make it colorful and eye-catching.
7. Write rules and directions on how to play your game.

Rules and How to Play

- How does a player move around the board? Here are some ideas:
  - roll the number cubes
  - pick up a card and answer a question
  - follow the instructions on the game board spaces
- How many people can play?
- Are there penalties for wrong answers?

Ideas for Game Cards

- math questions
- true or false
- answer the question
- multiple choice

continued next page ☞

Create game cards for your board game.

continued next page ☞

BLM 52

start

finish

continued next page ☞

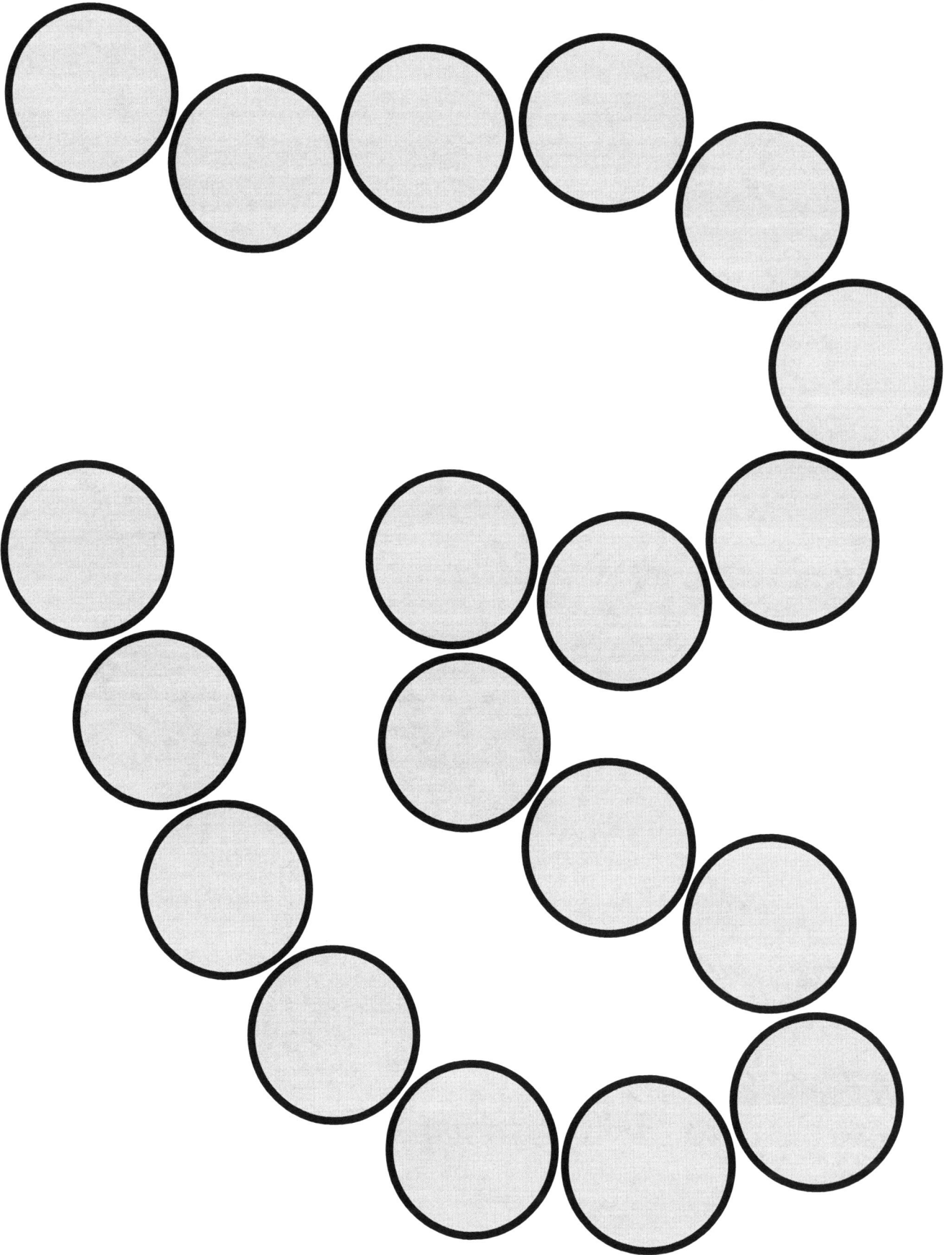

NEWS STORY

Use this planner to write a news story about an event from real life or from a story.

Headline _____

Who is the story about?

_____

_____

What happened?

_____

_____

Where did it happen?

_____

_____

When did it happen?

_____

_____

A Web Organizer About...

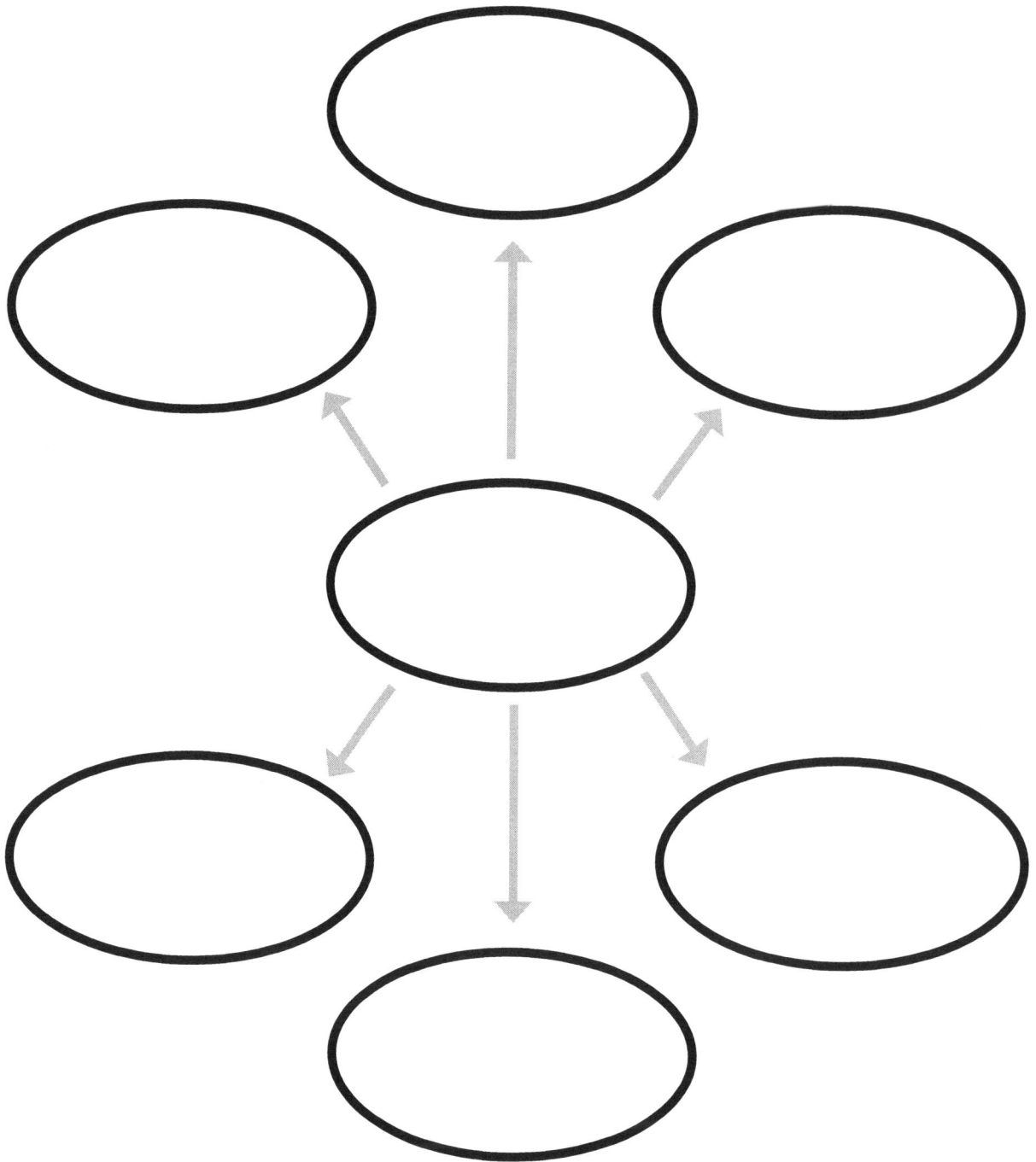

_____

Comparison Chart

Information

Comparing

Information

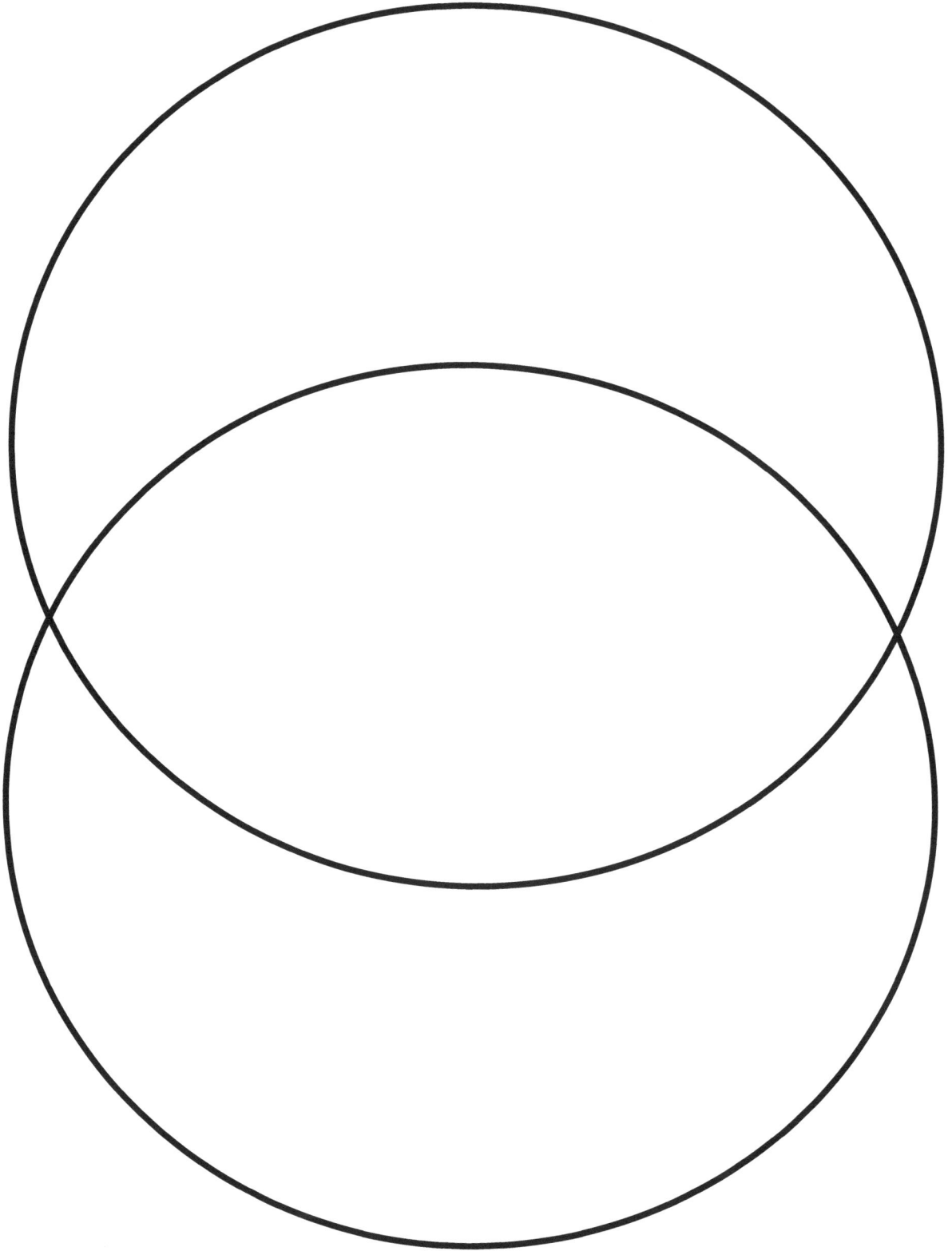

Venn Diagram

GO 3

Media Expert!

_____

You are unbelievable!

Great Work!

_____

Keep up the effort!

Rubric 1: Oral Presentation

	Level 1 Below Expectations	Level 2 Approaching Expectations	Level 3 Meets Expectations	Level 4 Exceeds Expectations
Presentation Style	• Infrequently uses gestures, eye contact, and tone of voice to engage the audience. • Does not hold the attention of the audience. • Is not prepared.	• Sometimes uses gestures, eye contact, and tone of voice to engage the audience. • Holds the attention of the audience for some of the presentation. • Is somewhat prepared and lacks confidence.	• Usually uses gestures, eye contact, and tone of voice to engage the audience. • Holds the attention of the audience for most of the presentation. • Is well prepared and confident.	• Successfully uses gestures, eye contact, and tone of voice to engage the audience. • Holds the attention of the audience for all of the presentation. • Is thoroughly prepared and confident.
Purpose	• Purpose of the presentation is not established. • The message is unclear.	• Purpose of the presentation is somewhat apparent. • The message is somewhat clear.	• Purpose of the presentation is apparent. • The message is clear.	• Purpose of the presentation is clear. • The message is obviously clear.
Content	• Exhibits little content knowledge. • Content lacks organization and contains abrupt transitions.	• Exhibits limited content knowledge. • Content is somewhat organized with few evident transitions.	• Shows content knowledge. • Content is organized with evident transitions.	• Shows thorough content knowledge. • Content is organized with fluid transitions.
Assignment Requirements	• Assignment requirements are incomplete.	• More than half of the assignment requirements are fulfilled.	• Assignment requirements are fulfilled.	• Assignment requirements are fulfilled in extended ways.

Rubric 2: Brilliant Brochure

	Level 1 Below Expectations	Level 2 Approaching Expectations	Level 3 Meets Expectations	Level 4 Exceeds Expectations
Content	• Less than half of the sections in the brochure are complete. • Little of the content is accurate.	• More than half of the sections in the brochure are complete. • The content is accurate to a certain extent.	• Almost all of the sections in the brochure are complete. • All of the content is accurate.	• Each section of the brochure is complete. • All of the content is accurate with added detail.
Brochure Appeal	• Brochure layout is not organized and is confusing for the reader.	• Brochure layout is fairly organized.	• Brochure layout is organized and eye-catching.	• Brochure layout is very organized and very eye-catching.
Purpose	• Purpose of the brochure is not established. • The message is unclear.	• Purpose of the brochure is somewhat apparent. • The message is somewhat clear.	• Purpose of the brochure is apparent. • The message is clear.	• Purpose of the brochure is obvious. • The message is obviously clear.
Visual Elements	• Very few graphics support the information.	• Some graphics support the information.	• Most graphics support the information.	• Graphics successfully support the information.
Proofreading	• There are several spelling or grammar errors.	• There are some spelling or grammar errors.	• There are few spelling or grammar errors.	• There are no spelling or grammar errors.

Rubric 3: Poster

	Level 1 Below Expectations	Level 2 Approaching Expectations	Level 3 Meets Expectations	Level 4 Exceeds Expectations
Poster Appeal	• Poor design. Layout is unattractive and messy.	• Basic design. Layout and neatness are acceptable.	• Interesting design. Layout and neatness are good.	• Very well-thought-out design. Excellent layout and neatness.
Content	• Few facts are accurately displayed on the poster.	• Some facts are accurately displayed on the poster.	• Most facts are accurately displayed on the poster.	• Facts are accurately displayed on the poster.
Graphic Support	• No graphics are related to the topic and no support of the information.	• Few graphics are related to the topic and little support of the information.	• Most graphics are related to the topic and support the information.	• Graphics are related to the topic and support the information.
Assigned Poster Requirements	• Several elements were missing. No additional information was added.	• Some of the necessary elements are included, but no additional information.	• Most of the necessary elements are included, as well as some additional information.	• All necessary elements are included, as well as additional information.

Rubric 4: Media Concepts

	Level 1 Below Expectations	Level 2 Approaching Expectations	Level 3 Meets Expectations	Level 4 Exceeds Expectations
Student Participation	• Rarely contributes to class discussions and activities by offering ideas and asking questions.	• Sometimes contributes to class discussions and activities by offering ideas and asking questions.	• Usually contributes to class discussions and activities by offering ideas and asking questions.	• Consistently contributes to class discussions and activities by offering ideas and asking questions.
Understanding of Concepts	• Shows little understanding of concepts and rarely gives complete explanations. • Intensive teacher support is needed.	• Shows a satisfactory understanding of most concepts and sometimes gives appropriate, but incomplete explanations. • Teacher support is sometimes needed	• Shows a good understanding of most concepts and usually gives complete or nearly complete explanations. • Infrequent teacher support is needed.	• Shows a thorough understanding of all or almost all concepts and consistently gives appropriate and complete explanations independently. • No teacher support is needed.
Communication of Concepts	• Rarely communicates with clarity and precision in written and oral work, or uses appropriate terminology and vocabulary.	• Sometimes communicates with clarity and precision in written and oral work, and uses appropriate terminology and vocabulary.	• Usually communicates with clarity and precision in written and oral work, and uses appropriate terminology and vocabulary.	• Consistently communicates with clarity and precision in written and oral work, and uses appropriate terminology and vocabulary.

Media Concepts Class Evaluation

Student's Name	Class Participation	Understanding of Concepts	Communication of Concepts	Overall Evaluation

Media Literacy Vocabulary

Keep a list of new media literacy words you have learned.
Make sure to include the definition for each word.

Word	Definition

How Am I Doing?

	Completing my work	Using my time wisely	Following directions	Keeping organized
Full speed ahead!	• My work is always complete and done with care. • I added extra details to my work.	• I always get my work done on time.	• I always follow directions.	• My materials are always neatly organized. • I am always prepared and ready to learn.
Keep going!	• My work is complete and done with care. • I added extra details to my work.	• I usually get my work done on time.	• I usually follow directions without reminders.	• I usually can find my materials. • I am usually prepared and ready to learn.
Slow down!	• My work is complete. • I need to check my work.	• I sometimes get my work done on time.	• I sometimes need reminders to follow directions.	• I sometimes need time to find my materials. • I am sometimes prepared and ready to learn.
Stop!	• My work is not complete. • I need to check my work.	• I rarely get my work done on time.	• I need reminders to follow directions.	• I need to organize my materials. • I am rarely prepared and ready to learn.

Media Literacy Glossary

Advertising Calling attention to a product, service, need, etc. It is often a paid announcement on websites or billboards, over radio or television, or in newspapers or magazines.

Audience Intended consumers, listeners, readers, or viewers for a particular media text.

Bias Tendency or inclination. Bias may prevent a person from looking at an issue with an open mind.

Blogs Personal journals published on the Internet. Blog is short for *weblog*.

Brand loyalty A person's preference for a product. Companies work hard to make customers loyal to their products.

Browsers Software programs that let you find, see, and hear material on the Internet. Examples of browsers include Internet Explorer, Firefox, Safari, etc. Also called Web browsers.

CD-ROMs (Compact Disc Read-Only Memory) Computer discs that can store large amounts of information but cannot record or save it.

Chat rooms Branches of a computer network that allow participants to communicate in real-time discussions.

Connotations Descriptions of ideology, meaning, or value that are associated with media text.

Consumers People who buy goods or services and use them personally, rather than selling them.

Conventions Accepted practices or rules in the use of language. Conventions can include capital letters, punctuation, headings, etc. See also *text features*.

Critical thinking Ability to question and understand issues presented in advertisements, print, television, etc.

Cyberspace Electronic communication on the Internet and other computer networks, and the culture developing around them.

Deconstruct To break down a media text into its parts to understand how and why it was created.

Demographics Characteristics or data about a group of people, including age, gender, education, income, etc.

Digital media Electronic devices and media platforms on which people can create and store media texts, and interact with others. Digital media includes cell phones, computers, Internet, social networking websites, etc.

Discussion groups Online areas that are focused on specific topics. Users can read other people's comments and add their own comments.

Elements of text Characteristics of a specific text form, including characters, setting, story, and more.

Emails Messages sent electronically between computer users. *Email* stands for "electronic mail."

Emoticons Symbols people use in emails and chat rooms to show an emotion. For example, :) means "I am happy."

Facts Things that actually exist.

FAQs (Frequently Asked Questions) Questions and answers about a specific topic, such as mailing lists, products, websites, etc.

Flaming Insulting people or criticizing them angrily in an electronic message.

Focus groups Small groups of people chosen by marketers to test new advertisements, products, or services. Marketers use these groups to try to learn how a larger group will react.

Genre Media texts that have a specific content, form, or style.

Hardware Electrical, electronic, magnetic, and mechanical devices in a computer system, including the disk drives, keyboard, and screen.

Home pages Initial pages of websites on the Internet.

HTML (Hypertext Markup Language) Formatting or standards used in documents on the Internet.

Hyperlinks Links or cross-references from one electronic document to another electronic document or to a webpage.

Hypertext Method of storing data through a computer program that lets users make and link information.

Ideology Beliefs that guide a group or institution.

IM (Instant Messaging) System for exchanging typed electronic messages instantly via a cellular network or the Internet.

Industry Groups involved in the production of media texts.

Internet World's largest system of linked computers.

ISP (Internet Service Provider) Company that can connect you directly to the Internet.

Jolts Moments in a media text generated by comedy, loud noises, rapid editing, and more. These jolts are included to interest and excite the audience.

Marketing The many ways products are sold. Marketing includes advertising, selling, and delivering products to people.

Mass media Communication aimed at a very large audience. Mass media includes the Internet, magazines, television, and more.

Media Forms of communication, including CD-ROMs, magazines, television, and websites. (*Media* is the plural of *medium*.)

Media conventions and techniques Creating specific effects using images and sounds to convey the message in a text. Examples of effects include using animation, color, logos, special effects, and more.

Media education Learning how to create media texts, as well as how to interpret them.

Media forms Formats used to communicate a message. Media forms can include blogs, movies, product packaging, and more.

Media literacy Understanding of media and the techniques used by them.

Media texts Images, sound, text, or visuals (or combinations of these) that are used to communicate a message.

Medium Form of communication, such as the Internet, radio, or television. (The plural of *medium* is *media*.)

Multimedia Combination of two or more forms of media, such as audio, images, text, and video.

Narratives Telling of a plot or story. In a media text, narrative is the coherent sequence of events.

Net All of cyberspace, including commercial services, the Internet, etc.

Netiquette Rules of behavior or etiquette that apply when using computer networks, especially the Internet.

Newbies New users of a technology.

Online communication Communicating over the Internet or through a commercial network.

Opinions Attitudes or beliefs, often not based on facts.

Point of view Attitude or opinion. Point of view affects how events are acted on or seen.

Posting Sending an electronic message to a discussion group or other message area.

Print and electronic resources Information or reference materials that are in print or electronic media. These resources include books, databases, videos, and more.

Print media Any media text produced on paper. Can also include such usages as a blimp with a company logo, and may contain only photographs without words.

Product placement Advertising that involves marketers paying to have their product shown in the media.

Production Process of creating media texts. Also, the people who create media texts.

Representation Process of media texts describing and standing for ideas, people, places, or real events.

Search engines Programs on some websites that can search for information on the Internet, based on supplied words or phrases.

Servers Computers that provide data or software programs to other machines linked to it in a network.

Social networks Online communities of people who use a website or other technologies to communicate.

Software Programs used to direct the operation of computers. Systems software, such as Mac OS and Windows, operate computers. Application software has such uses as playing games, word processing, etc.

Spam Unwanted email on the Internet.

Stereotypes Simplified, standardized images of people or things.

Storyboards Sequences of sketches used to plan an advertisement, movie, television show, or video.

Target audience Specific group of people expected to buy a particular product or service.

Technology Machinery, materials, and tools used to create a media text. Technology can have a big impact on the connotation and construction of a media text.

Text Communication that uses words, sounds, or images to present information. Can be in electronic, oral, print, or visual form. Also, to send a text message.

Text features Characteristics of a text that clarify the text, including fonts, headings, and illustrations. See also *conventions*.

Text messages Usually very short messages sent electronically. Text messages often contain short forms and emoticons.

URL (Uniform Resource Locator) Address of a website on the Internet.

Values Personal views or judgments about what is important in life.

Webcasts Broadcasts or recordings of events on the Internet.

Webpages Pages of information at a website. Webpages can include graphics, hyperlinks, text, and more.

WebQuests Inquiries in which most or all of the information gathered is drawn from the Internet.

Websites Collections of webpages. These pages may include graphics, sounds, and links to other websites. A website may cover one topic or many topics.

Answers to BLM Questions

Media Forms Word Search (p. 9)

T	P	O	S	T	E	R	W	E	C
B	I	L	L	B	O	A	R	D	O
E	A	S	T	B	O	O	K	W	M
M	D	O	S	I	G	N	A	E	M
A	W	N	S	M	E	N	U	B	E
P	S	G	C	O	M	I	C	S	R
P	I	C	T	U	R	E	T	I	C
M	A	G	A	Z	I	N	E	T	I
E	C	A	R	D	A	S	T	E	A
N	E	W	S	P	A	P	E	R	L

BLM 4: All About Media Forms (p. 13)

1. Sample answers: Media is television programs and commercials; books, newspapers, and magazines; signs in the community; and songs and programs on the radio. Students may also suggest letters, notes, textbooks, picture books, coloring books, websites, advertisements, sale ads, cards, comic books, newsletters, and posters.

2. Sample answers: Coloring books have black outlines of pictures that people color in, whereas picture book have photographs or pictures that are usually in color. Coloring books have little or no text, whereas picture books have more text. Coloring books often do not tell a story or give information, whereas picture books tell a story or give information. Coloring books have soft covers, whereas picture books can have a soft or hard cover. **Note:** The questions on this page encourage students to use the characteristics of media forms to distinguish between them. As a follow-up, you might consider asking students to point out characteristics that allow them to distinguish between other media forms, such as stories and poems, and newspapers and magazines. Where possible, provide examples of the media forms for students to examine.

BLM 5: Signs and Symbols (p. 14)

1. **a)** No dogs are allowed here. **b)** It is now safe to walk across the street. **c)** This is poisonous. **d)** This is wheelchair accessible or for people who use a wheelchair. **e)** Both women and men can use this washroom. **f)** Stop at a red light, slow down for a yellow light, or go when the light is green. **g)** Do not drop your trash on the ground. **h)** No smoking.

BLM 7: What Is the Internet? (p. 17)

1. Answers will vary.
2. Answers will vary.
3. Telephone and mail; telephone is faster

BLM 9: We Send and Receive Messages (p. 21)

1. **a)** Jane **b)** Jane **c)** Tom

BLM 16: What Is a Purpose? (p. 43)

Answers will vary.

BLM 17: Media Purposes (pp. 44–45)

1. To convince people want to buy something (the toy robot). Another purpose is to make money for the people who are selling the toy.
2. To give information on how to make the food.
3. **a)** *Comic book*—Let people have fun.
   b) *Newspaper*—Give information. **c)** *Radio weather report*—Give information. **d)** *Movie*—Let people have fun. **e)** *Television game show*—Let people have fun. **f)** *Map*—Give information. **g)** *Menu*—Give information. **h)** *Song*—Let people have fun.
   Note: Students might also suggest that comic strips in newspapers let people have fun, or that some movies give information such as how people lived long ago. Confirm, when appropriate, that these ideas are correct. Then explain that this activity focuses on the main, or usual, purpose of various media forms.

BLM 18: What Is the Purpose? (p. 46)
2. a) A recipe for cookies—Inform **b)** A cartoon—Entertain **c)** A report in the newspaper about a hockey game—Inform **d)** An advertisement about a new type of running shoe—Persuade **e)** A television commercial about a new movie—Entertain **f)** A video game about a frog—Entertain.
Note: Students may also say that newspaper report about a hockey game can entertain through the writer's commentary, the running shoe ad can entertain through pictures of people doing funny or amazing things, and the commercial about a movie can persuade people to go see the movie. Confirm, when appropriate, that these ideas are correct. Then explain that this activity focuses on the main, or usual, purpose of various media forms.

BLM 19: Media—What Is the Purpose? (p. 47)
Students should draw a happy face beside The Adventures of Jimmy Rabbit book, and a ? for the Animals of the Forest book, the Come to Our Field Day invitation, and The Life Cycle of a Frog diagram.
Note: Students may say the Animals of the Forest book can entertain by letting children have fun reading about the animals, and the Come to Our Field Day invitation can entertain by persuading children to participate and have fun. Confirm, when appropriate, that these ideas are correct. Then explain that this activity focuses on the main, or usual, purpose of various media forms.

BLM 20: What Is Advertising? (p. 49)
Answers to all questions will vary.

BLM 21: Convincing People to Buy a Product (pp. 51–52)
1. a) fact **b)** opinion **c)** opinion **d)** fact
2–4. Answers will vary.

BLM 23: Media Messages (p. 55)
1. Video of children looking bored as they played the game would send the message that the game is not fun to play.
2. Showing adults playing the game would send the message that the target audience for the game is adults.

3. Showing people having fun playing the game does not mean that everyone will enjoy the game. People do not all enjoy the same types of games, so not everyone will like this game. The game may be more enjoyable for children than adults. Some people may not enjoy playing board games.

BLM 25: Amazing Stories (p. 58)
1. Students should put a check mark beside "A boy plants a seed" and "The seed grows into a plant," and an X beside "The plant grows so tall that it touches the sky."
2. a) A girl gets a toy robot for her birthday. Her cat climbs onto her desk. **b)** A robot does homework. The cat speaks words to the girl.

BLM 28: Creating Media (p. 70)
1. Including a photograph of Pablo's pet goldfish is not a great idea because the goldfish is not part of the topic. Pablo's dog Sparky is the topic.
2. A good target audience would be students or children, since those are the groups that plays on the playground.
3. Answers will vary. Some students might suggest that a T-shirt is an effective choice of form because Sam's target audience of students will see the message on the T-shirt when Sam wears it to school. These students might feel that a brochure is not an effective choice of form because some students might not bother to read it. Other students may feel that a brochure would be a more effective form because it would allow Sam to include more information about recycling and why it is important, which would help to achieve Sam's purpose. These students may feel that a T-shirt is not a good choice of form. Many students might not notice the message, or might not be convinced that they should recycle paper just because Sam's T-shirt says they should. **Note:** A class discussion around this question and various opinions on it might help students to better understand why it is important to consider purpose and target audience when choosing a media form.